SPIRIT OF
INDIA

Front cover image:
Woman in sari standing near Taj Mahal
© Hugh Sitton/zefa/Corbis.

Back cover image:
Interior of Red Fort and Palace in Delhi
© Lucido Studio Inc./Corbis

First published in 2008
Parragon
Queen Street House
4 Queen Street
Bath BA1 1HE, UK

Copyright © Parragon Books Ltd 2008

Designed, produced, and packaged by Stonecastle Graphics Ltd

Text by Gill Davies
Designed by Sue Pressley and Paul Turner
Edited by Philip de Ste. Croix
Picture research by Karen James

ISBN 978-1-4075-2446-7

Printed in China

Author's note
The numbers of species, sizes of forests, and populations of cities
vary greatly from one reference source to another – no doubt
reflecting the fact that this is a fast-changing scenario and that
accurate numbers are difficult to determine at any one point in
time. The figures quoted in this book are intended to give a
feeling of the amazing diversity and richness of India but may
well be challenged by other sources. Readers must be aware that,
as with the rest of the world, acres of forest succumb to logging
or fire each week, species disappear at an alarming rate, and
people continually migrate from one place to another. The
situation is fluid and continually liable to change.

SPIRIT OF
INDIA

An exotic land of history, culture and color

Gill Davies

PaRragon

Bath · New York · Singapore · Hong Kong · Cologne · Delhi · Melbourne

CONTENTS

INTRODUCTION

'India is the cradle of the human race, the birthplace of human speech, the mother of history, the grandmother of legend, and the great grandmother of tradition.
... nothing has been left undone, either by man or nature, to make India the most extraordinary country that the sun visits on his rounds.'

Mark Twain, American writer and journalist (1835-1910)

This is an exotic place, a land and a culture that oozes rich colors and vibrancy, a land of great contrasts that is subject to searingly hot summers, pelting monsoon downpours, and freezing conditions bringing ice and snow in its loftier climes. This is a nation of countless people – some going about their busy lives in bustling cities and seaside ports, others in smaller towns and scattered villages, along the shoreline, beside rushing rivers and high in the hills. India is a country of diverse landscapes – from gentle shores lapped by warm seas to hot steaming jungles, lofty mangrove forests, arid deserts, cooler rolling plains, high hills, and dramatic snow-clad mountain peaks.

Its vibrant jostling cities have evolved through a long and amazing history. Here, over the centuries, millions of people have met, mingled and their lives have flowed together to create an exuberant culture that (at today's estimates) comprises two thousand or so ethnic groups. This is a nation with a fascinating history that has been home to a continuous civilization since around 2500 BC. Its origins began long, long before that, however, for the earliest inhabitants arrived in this fertile triangle of land perhaps some 500,000 years ago. India welcomed and nourished these new arrivals, fed their minds and bodies, and nurtured them in a way that would, in due course, give rise to a myriad cultures.

The newcomers discovered fertile river valleys and abundant animal life. Eventually these hunter-gatherers settled and started to cultivate the land. Their tools and implements are still being uncovered in the Indus river valley, now considered one of the cradles of civilization. Long, long ago – some 5000 years past – an amazing early culture flourished here and it developed to become one of the globe's most influential civilizations.

In due course, states and empires emerged, religions met and impacted upon each other, borders shifted, kings and princes flourished. In the 3rd, 4th, and 5th centuries AD, northern India was unified under the Gupta Dynasty and entered its Golden Age when Hindu culture and political administration scaled new heights. Time flowed on. Invaders brought Islamic influence into the country, wealthy maharajas raised magnificent edifices … the Mughal and the British Empires poured their influences into the cultural melting pot … and history has many dramatic tales to tell. All this time, art and literature blossomed and scientific scholarship flourished. India's contribution to the development of medicine, for instance, is of enormous significance.

Now, with just over 1.1 billion inhabitants (estimated in September 2007), this great nation is runner-up in the world's largest population stakes – second only to China. It is home to about one-sixth of the world's people. India's inhabitants speak at least 17 different languages and almost 900 local dialects. This subcontinent was the birthplace of four great world religions – Hinduism, Buddhism, Jainism, and Sikhism. Over 80 percent of its inhabitants today are followers of the Hindu religion but there are also major groups of Muslims and Buddhists, as well as Jews, Christians, and several other religious sects.

Above: Beautiful henna decoration is applied for festivals and celebrations – especially weddings when a bride's hands (and feet) will be decorated with the most intricate designs, called mehndi.

Right: This colorful fresco encompasses much that is characteristic of India's glorious culture – its rich decorative flair, history, tradition and costumes, birds, flowers, and elephants.

Today the subcontinent boasts the world's most populous democracy. Other riches follow in the wake of this diversity of beliefs and historic heritage and India's great culture is reflected in her splendid architecture that includes stunning palaces, magnificent temples, powerful stupas (burial shrines), and serene monasteries. The Taj Mahal stands as a world-famous icon of romantic building, the encapsulation of emotion in gleaming white marble that subtly shifts its moods and tones under the changing light of sun and moon.

This is a land of so many contrasts – encompassing rural villages where women still set about their laundry on the riverbanks, keeping a watchful eye out for hungry crocodiles, and vibrant metropolitan cities that rival any in the world for their modernity. There are exotic bustling bazaars –where shoppers haggle over a brilliant array of colorful cloth and silks, jewelry, fruit, fish, and spices – as well as modern supermarkets and gleaming shopping malls.

Home to some 16 percent of the world's people, India also offers an equally amazing array of habitats to countless plants and animals. About 65 million years ago the tectonic plate bearing the Indian subcontinent collided with the Asian plate but it remained protected by the high Himalayan wall so its animals and plants retained a secure home in the landscape. While some new arrivals have infiltrated over the mountains or washed up on its shores, India remained a devoted mother to many very special creatures and plants – its rich forests and plains encouraging these to flourish, while those species that did manage to invade served to add most colorfully to the nation's own natural diversity.

Scientists estimate that at least 13,000 species of flowering plants and more than 65,000 kinds of animals live in this glistening landscape. This wonderfully rich ecology is reflected in its culture too, inspiring many works of art and literature and being woven into many a myth and legend. India's national bird is the brilliant peacock, its national animal the prowling tiger, and its national flower the delicious, dreamy lotus. All are beautiful – as splendid as the nation they represent. This is the land of the ever-rarer Asian elephant, elusive snow leopards, sloth bears, Asiatic lions, the great Indian rhinoceros, and many chattering monkeys that clamber in the trees. In the oceans that sweep around India's crinkled shoreline are great manta rays, whales, and sea snakes. Meanwhile, inland, a myriad reptiles include almost 400 snake species, such as the Indian python, krait and king cobras whose glistening coils unravel to an amazing 12ft (3 to 4m) in length.

There are problems associated with this glorious Noah's Ark, of course. The entire natural world is coming under increasing pressure, right around the globe, and the land of the tiger is no exception to this crisis. Forests have become fragmented, rivers have been dammed or polluted, sea life has been damaged or its biodiversity depleted, species disappear all too quickly. India is losing parts of its flora and fauna at an alarming rate – in particular the magnificent tigers for there are now fewer than 3000 specimens left prowling in the wild. However, vast areas do remain unspoiled and protection programs have been put in place to save India's threatened environment and species. National parks and wildlife sanctuaries cover a vast area of the landscape encompassing many vital biospheres and tiger reserves, but tigers still vanish at an alarming rate.

India seems destined to overwhelm all five senses with its glorious scenery, colorful festivals and costumes, with the scents and flavors of spices and magnificent Indian cuisine, with the rhythm of its evocative music and of pelting monsoon rains, and with the warmth of the sun beating down on this splendid land.

Opposite: *Dusk casts a purple haze over historic bustling Mumbai, where new and old buildings vie for attention in the so-called 'city of gold' – home to the Bollywood movies.*

Left: *The old 'blue city' of Jodhpur is surrounded by a thick stone wall. Situated near the geographic center of Rajasthan, it is rich with fine palaces, forts, temples, and bazaars and is a popular tourist destination.*

COASTS AND ISLANDS

The map of India is a dominant shape on the atlas, an immediately recognizable triangle, seeming to melt down to its tip and point at the 'drip' of Sri Lanka that, in fact, lies beyond India's frontiers. This striking outline draws the eye inward and so it is sometimes easy to overlook the many islands that belong to the nation too and which, like a sprinkle of exotic spice, pepper the nearby seas and add to the habitat diversity populated by an already vibrant aquatic wildlife.

COASTS AND ISLANDS

The triangular outline of this exciting nation is edged by several seas and the vast expanse of the mighty Indian Ocean that washes around its irregular contours. Rains sweep in from the southwest during June to October, and then, especially from October to December, the coast may be buffeted by fierce storms and cyclones.

The Western Coastal Plain is a narrow strip set beside the Arabian Sea, that runs from Gujarat in the north to Kerala in the south. It is inundated by small rivers flowing swiftly down from the Western Ghats mountains to form estuaries near the sea. India's most southerly land feature is Indira Point in the Nicobar islands, which lie some way to the east of the subcontinent facing toward Sumatra. At the southern tip of India itself is Kanyakumari, which is where the Indian Ocean, the Bay of Bengal, and the Arabian Sea meet. Hindus consider a bath in this marine confluence as especially sacred and the October Cape Festival held here celebrates the only place in India where sunset and moonrise can be viewed simultaneously on the day of a full moon.

Above: A traditional fishing boat slides through still waters. India has 1864 miles (3000km) of coastline where the fish include sharks, barracuda, blue marlin, tiger prawns, tuna, and groupers.

Right: Birds wade at the tidal edge as waves turn silver and pink in a sunset glow – but the weather and tidal conditions around India's coastline are not always as peaceful as this.

The eastern coastline drops down beside the Bay of Bengal and is flanked by the Eastern Ghats as it wriggles down from West Bengal to Tamil Nadu. It is sprinkled with plains and river deltas. Rice is an important crop here, especially in the fertile 'rice bowl' of Orissa. This is a crop that has been grown for more than 5000 years and it remains vital to India's economy, its cultivation providing employment for vast numbers of people. It is served at almost every meal.

Fishing has long been important too and at August's first full moon the Nariyal or Coconut Pournima festival is celebrated along both eastern and western coasts by fishermen who feast on coconut sweets and pray to the sea god, seeking permission to return to the ocean to fish and asking for a good season's catch – vital for their livelihoods.

The Arabian Sea

The western coast of India is lapped by the warm salty waves of the Arabian Sea, the northwest part of the Indian Ocean. To the north the mighty Indus river broadens as its estuary meets the ocean near Karachi in Pakistan. Farther south the most important port is Mumbai (Bombay), which for centuries has been a vital link in the trade routes between Europe and India. At its broadest point, the Arabian Sea is about 1500 miles (2400km) wide as it washes from the Indian coast to the shores of the Arabian Peninsula.

This is an area of teeming coral reefs, sea grass beds where mollusks thrive, sand and mud strands, forests of kelp, and lofty mangrove swamps. Barracuda, wrasse, and damselfish dance through the waters. Dugongs, turtles, dolphins, and finless porpoises swim, manta rays move sinuously though the water, squid, cuttlefish, and octopuses wave their tentacles and there are whale sharks as well as giant sperm, blue, and humpback whales – the giants of the ocean.

Right: *A humpback whale breaches, a dramatic sight. The males are also famous for their loud complex 'songs' and vocalizations used to herd fish into their bubble 'nets' that whales release in the water to encircle their prey and prevent them from escaping their cavernous jaws.*

Opposite: *Silvery barracuda marked with strong 'cross-bar' stripes: they can grow up to 6ft (1.8m) or more in length and are voracious hunters with fearsome fang-like teeth.*

The Bay of Bengal

The eastern edge of India's land mass curves around the Bay of Bengal with the Andaman Sea lying farther to the east. This is the northeastern segment of the Indian Ocean and, like India itself, it is triangular in shape. Its relatively shallow waters cover an area of some 839,000sq miles (2,173,000km²). A number of large rivers, including the Ganges and Brahmaputra, flow into the Bay of Bengal and they form fertile deltas as the river sediment creates shallow bays along the shore.

A popular Bengali saying 'Baro Mase Tero Parban' refers to 13 festivals held in 12 months and is an indication of the plethora of such events here. Naba Barsho marks the start of the Bengali year and celebrates trade with flowers, offerings at temples and visits to newly decorated shops. At Rathayatra, which is held at Mahesh in June or July, there is a week-long festival when people help to pull the roped chariots of Hindu deities Lord Jagannath, Balaram, and Subhadra, taking them to and from the temple.

The Bay of Bengal has coral reefs and mangroves aplenty. Many fish spawn here while turtles, sea snakes, whales, marlin, barracuda, tuna, and dolphins live in coastal waters. While generally warm and hospitable, this area can also be subject to battering monsoon rains, devastating cyclone storms and, in an area of shifting tectonic plates, earthquakes, volcanoes, and tsunami as the India Plate slowly moves northeast.

Above: A traditional fishing boat, seen here on a beach at sunset.

Left: Barefoot fishermen attend to their boats in the Bay of Bengal, one of the world's greatest marine ecosystems.

The Indian Ocean

India's southern tip juts into the mighty Indian Ocean, a vast body of salt water that – albeit the smallest and youngest of the world's three major oceans – covers about one-fifth of the total ocean area of the world. It stretches for over 6200 miles (10,000km) between the southern tips of Africa and Australia, encompassing about 28,360,000sq miles (73,440,000km²).

Here are diverse coral reefs, predatory sharks, blue-ringed octopuses, crown of thorns sea stars, and turtles. Saltwater or estuarine crocodiles (*Crocodylus porosus*) thrive – some reach huge proportions measuring over 18ft (5.5m) in length and they may weigh almost a ton. These mighty beasts live in tidal estuaries and marine swamps, in brackish coastal waters and the lower reaches of rivers from Cochin on the west coast to the Sundarbans in West Bengal through to the Andaman Islands. Highly aggressive, they may well have given rise to some of the ancient legends of sea monsters and dragons.

The Sumatra-Andaman seas are subject to undersea earthquakes and this was the site of the devastating December 2004 tsunami that surged across the Indian Ocean. In places the waves were nearly 33ft (10m) high and at least 16,000 people died in the coastal regions of India.

Above: The statue of Thiruvalluvar, a celebrated Tamil poet, at Kanyakumari, the most southern point of India where the Arabian Sea, the Bay of Bengal, and the Indian Ocean come together.

Opposite above: Cochin fishermen busily attend to their ropes and nets. One of India's largest fishing fleets is found here, with over 400 trawlers based in the area.

Left: A saltwater crocodile gapes – the largest crocodilian, males reach about 17ft (5m) or more and weigh at least 1000lb (450kg).

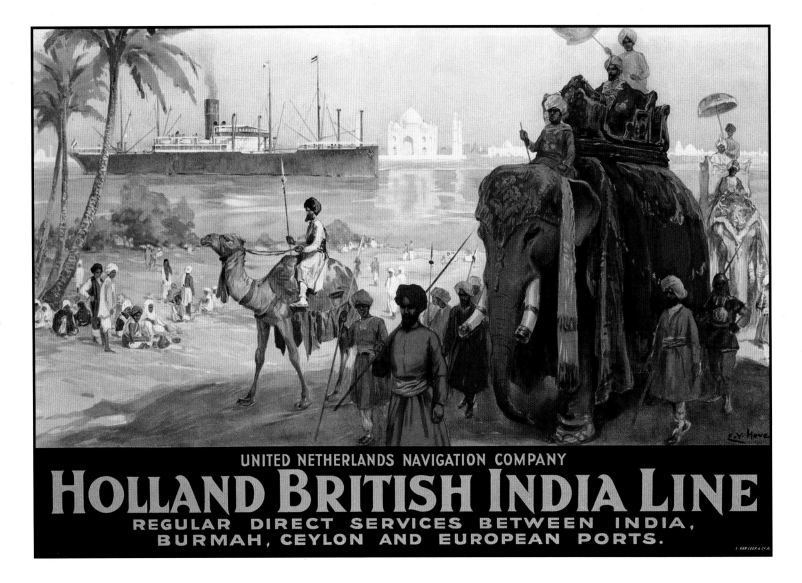

UNITED NETHERLANDS NAVIGATION COMPANY
HOLLAND BRITISH INDIA LINE
REGULAR DIRECT SERVICES BETWEEN INDIA, BURMAH, CEYLON AND EUROPEAN PORTS.

Ocean history and the rise of trade

Ever a busy place, from about 3000 BC, merchant ships bustled along the coasts here voyaging between southern Arabia and India, carrying teakwood from India and incense from Arabia to trade for wheat, cheese, and barley. Today, a less romantic but equally rich cargo load is the 100,000 tons of oil that tankers routinely ferry across the waters between Mukalla in Yemen and Mumbai (Bombay).

India's rich maritime history boasts the world's first-ever tidal dock, built in Lothal, a prominent city in the Indus valley civilization established some 4500 years ago. It lies close to modern Ahmadabad in Gujarat state. Ships from this harbor and other ancient Indian ports established trade with Mesopotamia and the Persians and became the center of a thriving commerce in beads, gems, and fine ornaments. Archaeological excavations have revealed that Lothal scientists used a ring-like shell compass and may well have been the first to study stars and navigation some two millennia before the Greeks. The ancient site was not discovered until 1954.

India's coasts have long been a place of trade. It is believed that the Egyptians explored the northwestern fringes of the Indian Ocean as early as 2900 BC to 2200 BC. There is no definitive record of their crossing the treacherous waters but Indian products were known to them and the Bible describes King Solomon's fleet bringing back treasures that may well have come from India. Perhaps 'his shipmen that had knowledge of the sea' were sent to discover the gold, silver, and precious gems of this exotic land of strutting peacocks and glittering serpents.

The first Greek to have visited India and written an account of it is reputed to have been Skylax of Karyanda in the 5th century BC. What is beyond dispute is that in 327 BC the Greek king and military commander Alexander the Great, having subdued Syria, Egypt, and Persia, marched on to invade the Punjab, the land of the five rivers, ruled by King Porus. Despite being confronted by war elephants, Alexander's fearless soldiers held sway for a brief spell until the war-weariness of his troops forced him to turn back toward Arabia. Thereafter India seems to have become a distant dream, off the map to all but the most fearless traders for many a long year.

Above: It was the strong demand for valuable Asian spices that stimulated many voyagers and merchants to discover new routes to the East.

Opposite: This advertisement promotes the services of a European shipping company. During colonial times, many were established in order to transport sought-after Indian goods to Europe.

Right: This ancient cannon bears a facial decoration. Many forbidding forts were built by the Dutch, French, British, and Portuguese to guard the coast.

In about 118 BC, Egypt heard first-hand of India's treasures from an Indian sailor discovered by Red Sea coastguards. After being presented to Ptolemy VIII Physcon (a nickname meaning Potbelly or Bladder), this shipwrecked survivor guided Eudoxus, a Greek navigator in Ptolemy's employ, back to his native shores. Eudoxus returned with a cargo of aromatic spices, perfumes and precious stones – the route to India was open.

According to legends, trade with the East was boosted in about AD 15 when a sea captain named Hippalus studied the monsoon patterns and realized that these powerful winds and currents could help to sweep vessels across the Indian Ocean. He is said to have discovered a sea route from the Red Sea to southern India.

A brisk trade was established as the ancient Greeks and Romans rushed to buy Chinese silk and a vast trade in Indian luxuries almost bankrupted the Roman treasury to the extent that the Senate discussed banning the use of Indian cotton for togas. In time, Arab connections with the East via India grew apace. European knowledge of Asia was extended during the Crusades and further augmented by the journeys of missionaries and explorers like Marco Polo. Chinese maritime trading in the Bay of Bengal dates from around the 1100s.

Even in the most ancient times, India's Mauryan Empire had been justifiably proud of its fine ships and the first scientific study of navigation began on the Indus river some 5000 years ago. Centuries later, the Chola dynasty (that dominated southern India from the 800s until the 1200s) boasted great shipbuilding and navigational expertise. Sea trade flourished and, ultimately, India's maritime expertise would help to spread its civilization (and Hinduism and Buddhism) as far as the islands of Java, Sumatra, Indonesia, and other southeast Asian countries.

Seafarers continued to take advantage of the monsoon winds and currents to assist their voyages. From the 9th to the 15th century, medieval Arab and Persian pilots described how they did this while navigating the oceans to reach India's ports. Long before the discovery of the Americas in 1492 (Columbus had actually set out to seek a new route to India), countless intrepid sailors from Europe were exploring India's coast, making

considerable voyages in fragile craft in search of prized trade routes and the riches of the East, seeking access to cotton, pepper, and valuable spices, such as cinnamon.

When Constantinople fell to the Ottoman Turks in 1453, Muslim traders were able to control the Black Sea trading posts and all the overland trails. Now European merchants desperately needed to find new routes to gain access to precious goods from the East. The stage was set for Portuguese explorer, Vasco da Gama. He famously opened up the sea route from Europe, sailing from Lisbon in 1497, negotiating the Cape of Good Hope to sail around Africa, cross the Indian Ocean and reach the south-western shores of India at Calicut in May 1498. He disproved the notion that the Indian Ocean was enclosed, set up colonies, subjugated the locals, and seized control of the spice trade. The sea voyage was much longer than overland trade routes but ocean travel was cheaper and, despite the possibility of piracy, avoided the much greater risk posed by bandits on lonely land routes.

Soon English, Dutch, and French ships were probing the oceans and the medieval seas around India fairly bustled with explorers,

voyagers, and traders. In 1500, Portuguese Pedro Álvares Cabral became the first European to discover the route to Brazil when his vessel explored the lands to the west during a voyage to India. After shipwrecks at the Cape of Good Hope and fights with Muslim traders in India, Cabral established supply routes for the transportation of Indian spices before returning to Portugal. Ten years later, Afonso de Albuquerque sailed to the Spice Islands (the Indonesian Moluccas), destroying the city of Calicut and seizing Goa for Portugal. The European colonization had truly begun.

Above: *As well as modern cargo ships, many local merchant vessels sail into Mumbai (Bombay), a natural harbor with three main docks and an important staging post for Indian trade.*

Opposite: *Kerala lies on the tropical Malabar coast in southwestern India where long ago many merchants from west Asia and southern Europe established trading posts. Here, huge ocean-going vessels dwarf a local rowing boat.*

The coast today

A cruise around India would include visits to many famous ports and cities sprinkled along this coastline, but while these are indeed important hubs of activity, in fact the majority of India's population (some 70 percent) still live in villages.

In a long inlet just south of the Pakistan border is the Gulf of Kutch Marine National Park in an Arabian Sea inlet that measures about 458sq miles (1186km^2) in area. Here, in an archipelago of 42 islands, dugongs and finless porpoises slip through a strange landscape of fringing coral reefs and 200 kinds of sponge, while on the beach, sea turtles haul themselves out to nest. Leatherback, olive ridley, and green turtles are encountered there while some 30 species of migratory birds seek shelter in the mangrove forests of the northwest coast, waiting until the worst storms pass before they fly onward.

Above: Karnataka, once the site of some of India's most powerful ancient empires, has a 200-mile (320km) long coastline. Its lovely beaches include five at Gokarna, a temple town.

Right: The large and endangered green turtle is generally sighted off India's western shores, rather than on its eastern side. Sadly, many die after becoming entangled in fishing nets.

Above: A horse-drawn taxi in Mumbai where the historic sights include many majestic colonial buildings and the streets are full of vendors and snake charmers all eager to catch the attention of passers-by.

Top: The Gateway of India at Mumbai port, a renowned sight at the edge of the sea with its sturdy arches and minarets inspired by medieval Gujarati architecture.

The Mumbai area

Mumbai (formerly Bombay) is India's largest city and biggest port – a busy, bustling place with a dense population and the most crowded, industrialized, and westernized city in India. This is both a commercial capital and industrial powerhouse. It is a city of contrasts – fine streets and palatial homes rub shoulders with sidewalk dwellers and tiny houses crowded together along dirt roads. The city rose on seven swampy islands that created a natural harbor – a good place to fish and moor vessels, ultimately leading to its role as a port and shipbuilding center presided over by a colonial fort. Today it houses an exhilarating mix of bustling bazaars, glittering shopping malls, Victorian mansions, and skyscrapers.

Perhaps its most famous landmark, the Gateway of India, a triumphal arch commemorating the visit of King George V and Queen Mary stands next to the red-domed Taj Mahal Hotel. Both are intricately carved and embellished – as is the Victoria Terminus (now called Chhatrapati Shivaji), a superb example of Victorian Gothic architecture: this is where Asia's first train departed from in 1853.

Mumbai is an amalgam of different faiths and places of worship – from the stunning white Haji Ali mosque on a causeway

projecting into the Arabian Sea to Christian churches, including St Thomas' Cathedral in the heart of the Fort area, the Jain Temple on Malabar Hill, and the Hindu's Mumba Devi Temple at Bhuleshwar in south Mumbai.

Among Mumbai's most famous sights are the 7th-century cave temples on Elephanta Island. They are carved out of the hillside to honor the god Shiva and are approached by a columned veranda flanked by sculptured elephants. Inside are magnificent carvings, including a great sculpture of Lord Shiva. A winter dance festival is held on this lovely island where monkeys scamper about, snatching food from visitors if the opportunity arises. The fishing village of Worli, in south Mumbai, is over 600 years old, jutting out into the sea and encompassing a small Portuguese port. It is now home to the impressive, honeycombed Nehru Center.

Local industries include the cultivation of cotton, sugar, strawberries, and mangoes. All along the coast that extends south from Mumbai are coconut groves, spice plantations, and villages where fishermen have hauled in their nets for more than 2000 years. In the monsoon-swept lands that loom beyond are found waterlogged paddy fields, plantations of cashew, betel nut, and rubber trees. The village houses characteristically have steeply sloping roofs to carry away the heaviest torrents of rain.

Above: A bicycle laden with coconuts. Mumbai developed on seven swampy islands. It was first colonized by the Portuguese in 1534 who called it Bom Bahia (meaning Good Bay).

Top: A busy Mumbai street, just one of the many crowded bustling thoroughfares in this dynamic city – a cosmopolitan financial center and port set on a narrow promontory.

Bollywood

Mumbai is the center of India's film industry, nicknamed Bollywood. It has produced many more films than America's Hollywood and is the world's largest cinema industry – with its output enjoyed in every town across the nation. Originally inspired by the Lumière Brothers Cinématographe showing of six short films at Bombay's Watson's Hotel in 1896, H S Bhatavdekar was the first Indian to begin making films in Bombay. Now 1000 Bollywood movies a year achieve ticket sales of 3.6 billion. Usually romantic musical extravaganzas, glamorous and spectacular, they offer the audience a chance to escape from often difficult lives – and have a huge following.

Goa and beyond

As the coastline stretches south to Goa, where Portuguese merchants first landed in the 15th century, there are fine stretches of sand backed by coconut palms and elegant Indo-Portuguese-style mansions in an area that now attracts many tourists. Long beaches lie strewn with seashells; some have lagoons and hot springs. Behind many of them runs a wide belt of forest. High rainfall helps maintain the tropical backdrop, which sustains several unique trees and plants – some introduced by the Portuguese, including green chili, which is now a prominent ingredient in curries.

Goa is renowned for its rich variety of fish dishes, especially fish curry with rice. Coconut and coconut oil is widely used and an exotic vegetable stew, known as khatkhate, is a very popular festival dish.

The warm humid climate encourages moist deciduous vegetation that is home to a rich variety of birds, animals, and reptiles. Dolphins leap out of the water here while many creatures thrive in the ten percent of Goa that has been established as a wildlife reserve. At the Doctor Salim Ali bird sanctuary island, local and migratory birds revel in a mangrove swamp paradise named after a famous ornithologist. As well as coastal birds, coots, and pintails, there are flying foxes, jackals, crocodiles and countless fish, snakes, and insects.

The coastline sweeps on past Mangalore, which is studded with cashew-nut, pepper, and coffee plantations where whitewashed churches, mosques, and houses with terracotta roofs appear among the coconut palm groves. Arab merchants once used this port, and they were followed by the Portuguese and British.

Above: Built in 1652, the magnificent Cathedral of St. Catherine of Alexandria is the largest church in Asia. One of the most celebrated and ancient buildings of Goa, it is the mother church of all Goan Christians.

Opposite: Sunset and palms – the dream of carefree escape lures many tourists to Goa's shores, but there are also wonderful temples and wildlife reserves to visit.

Above: As well as its busier beaches, Goa's Konkan coast has many a quiet stretch populated with just a scattering of boats.

Right: Karnataka state borders the Arabian Sea. Here Maurya Empire founder, Emperor Chandragupta (born c.340 BC), sought peace.

Lakshadweep islands

Down to the southwest, some 125 miles (200km) offshore, lie the Lakshadweep islands, a coral paradise set among azure seas where 36 islands and islets are arranged among 12 atolls, three reefs, and five submerged banks that, since 1956, have been a Union Territory of India.

Bread fruit and wild almond flourish as sea grasses wave and shimmer in beach-side lagoons. Hermit crabs play hide-and-seek as they 'move house' into ever bigger shells, while in the water some 600 species of fish include bright parrot fish, butterfly fish, and surgeon fish that have fiercely sharp, erectile spines called 'scalpels' on each side of a tail that can be used as a weapon and cuts like a knife. Their small mouths nibble and scrape organisms from rocks and coral. Here the local (mainly Muslim) people grow coconuts and use their fibers to make rope, pillows, and mattresses but only ten of these many beautiful coral islands are inhabited by people. Wildlife, however, flourishes in sparkling blue lagoons, among the waving coconut palm trees – and in among the beautiful coral reefs.

Above: Hermit crabs – the most common crabs in the Lakshadweep islands – scurry across the silver crescent beaches toward the shade of coconut groves.

Right: Boatman and pole – some Kerala houseboats are made of planks tied together with coir rope and coated with black resin obtained from cashew-nut shells. No nails are used in the construction.

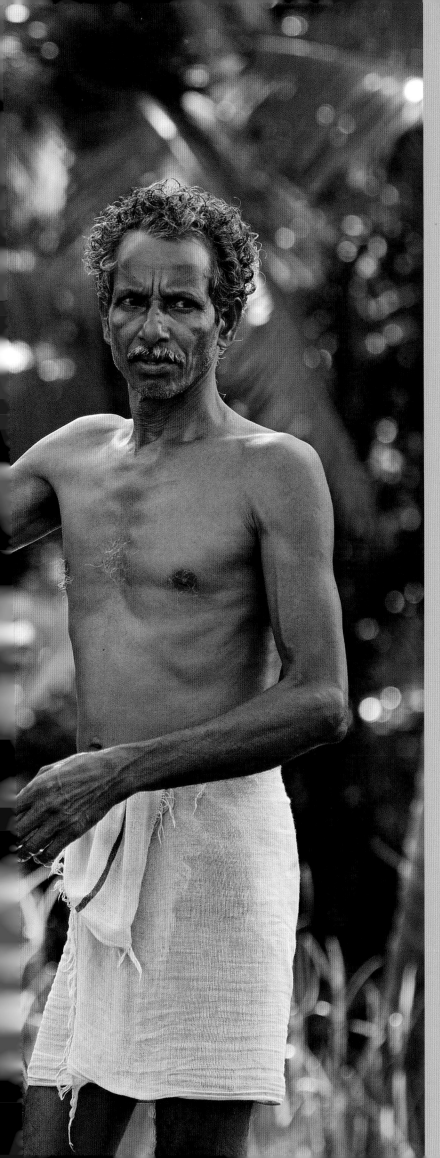

Kerala

Christianity arrived in Kerala at much the same time as it reached Europe – in AD 52 when St Thomas landed in the region. Today 20 percent of the population is Christian, 20 percent Muslim and some 60 percent Hindu. Kerala's coastline is lined with coconut trees and white sand. Here people are generally healthier and earn higher wages than in much of the rest of India due to enlightened land reform policies set in place over a century ago by princely rulers of what was then known as Travancore.

Kerala is renowned for its 560-mile (900km) length of sandy beaches and its many emerald backwaters, busy with wildlife, including estuarine and marshland crocodiles. With unspoiled tropical evergreen rainforests and lush trees, this state supports a wealth of land, marine, and avian wildlife and a wide variety of flora. Spice plantations grow cardamom, pepper, and tea. Inland the national parks are home to impressive mammals such as elephants and tigers, while the fringes are full of activity too, especially birdlife. Kerala is the place to see hornbills and kingfishers, storks, teals, egrets, herons, and darters.

The state capital Thiruvananthapuram (also known as Trivandrum) was named after the fabled serpent god 'Anantha' (on whom Lord Vishnu reclines) and is called the city of the snake god. Set by the sea, like Rome this is an ancient city built on seven hills – with a trading history dating back to 1000 BC.

Above: A houseboat cruises along Kerala's tranquil backwaters, discovering some of the secrets in this veritable network of lakes, canals, and 44 river estuaries.

Above: Many resorts in Kerala offer luxury accommodation amid lush landscapes and coconut palms (top). The Malabar 'Spice Coast' is edged by soft sandy beaches fringed with palms and here (above) their leaves are being transported by an elephant.

Right: Acres of tea plantations and fruit trees cloak the gentle Kerala hill slopes, with the neatly clipped tea bushes looking like massed emerald cushions stretching into the distance.

The southern tip

At the southeastern tip of India, the Gulf of Mannar national park and biosphere reserve encompasses islands, reefs, beaches, estuaries, tropical dry broadleaf forests, and salt marshes. Eleven species of sea grass, over 100 coral species, some 37 genera of hard coral, and 17 different mangrove species are found here. In one of the richest coastal regions in Asia, the marine national park supports over 3600 species of flora and fauna in a vast expanse of shallow waters and sometimes densely foliaged islands. The reef is home to pearl oysters and chank ('Indian conch' –*Turbinella pyrum*), a large, thick-shelled gastropod, as well as dolphins, herrings, barracuda, mollusks, sea anemones, crustaceans, sponges, sea horses, and many types of fish. Five species of turtle nest on the sandy shores while countless migratory birds soar overhead.

Here shallow sunlit water is full of seaweed and contorted corals appear in every shade from soft violet to vivid red. This fragile ecosystem may support as many as 3000 species in its crevices, fish nurseries, and breeding grounds. Meanwhile 12 sea grass genera also support their own marine communities. The area is busy with spinner and bottlenose dolphins as well as some highly endangered marine creatures, including dugongs or sea cows, many whales (toothed, baleen, blue, sei, fin, and pilot whales) and sausage-shaped sea cucumbers which are covered with warty bumps or soft spines. Sea cucumbers crawl across the sea floor on tiny suction-cup tube feet. They can contract their muscles to shoot water out and may even shoot out their insides to deter approaching predators and thus have to grow new ones. The Gulf of Mannar is probably the most biologically rich coastal region in India – or indeed in Asia, with amazingly diverse life in marine, shore, and tidal zones.

Wildlife also flourishes at the Point Calimere Sanctuary, in saline marshland south of Chennai (previously Madras). This is a swampy haven for many migratory birds. Water birds include gulls, flamingos, plovers, teals, and terns, but diverse habitats offer dry evergreen forests, salt marshes, mangrove vegetation, and grasslands as a home to many mammals too, such as blackbuck, wild boar, spotted deer, bonnet macaques, and jackals. Large groups of flying foxes cavort in the trees, while dolphins and turtles swim close to the shore.

Opposite left: A dolphin leaps close to the beach. Spinner and bottlenose dolphin inhabit the Gulf of Mannar but, along with dugongs and turtles, are sometimes snared in fishing nets.

Above: This superb coral reef is busy with brightly colored shoals of fish among the branches of coral. A clown fish is lurking by the anemones for greater protection.

Chennai

This hot, humid city, with a population of over 7 million people, is renowned for its temple architecture and vibrant culture. It hosts performances of classical Indian dance, a lively theater scene, colorful festivals, Hindu temples and the thriving Tamil film industry (dubbed Kollywood) that creates some 300 movies a year. There is a dynamic mix of ancient temples, old colonial buildings, and modern high-rise towers. This city was one of the first outposts of the British East India Company that built Fort St George in 1640 with its stern sloping ramparts and gun emplacements – now the seat of Tamil Nadu's government.

Many of Chennai's elegant buildings, such as the Egmore Railway Station and the University colleges, are rich ocher and red in color. There is traditional shopping to be found at the Pondy and Burma bazaars and many a good red madras curry can be enjoyed – it is made with lots of chili powder and is fairly hot. A typical Tamil meal consists of steamed rice served with up to six vegetable dishes, set on a banana leaf.

The city rose beside two rivers, the Cooum and the Adyar where the estuary region and its sandy banks provide a home for many birds and animals. Marina Beach, one of the world's longest, stretches for 8 miles (13km) and suffered badly when the 2004 tsunami caused many deaths and great destruction here.

Some 22 miles (35km) south of Chennai city, a wildlife reserve called Chennai Crocodile Bank has been set up to help stock the nation's wildlife sanctuaries and conserve endangered reptiles. Its lush vegetation and open pools are home to thousands of reptiles including turtles, monitor lizards, and saltwater crocodiles. These enormous 23ft (7m) long beasts weigh about 2200lb (1000kg) and live in brackish coastal waters and tidal river estuaries. With a fierce disposition, they have a reputation as man-eaters. They are intelligent and communicate by barks and calls, including a high-pitched distress call, warning hisses – and long, low growls and bellows during courtship.

Right: Locals claim that Chennai's Marina Beach, with a new lighthouse at the far end, is the longest straight stretch (8 miles) of urban beach in India. The Ice House on the beach drive once stored ice from North America's Great Lakes that was imported by ship for refrigeration purposes.

There is also a snake farm here where anti-venom is produced, potentially life-saving for anyone who has a confrontation with a king cobra *(Ophiophagus hannah)*. One of the most dangerous snakes, it lives near streams, forests, bamboo thickets, and dense mangrove swamps, growing to 18ft (5.5m) in length and with a head as big as a man's hand. The venom from one bite can kill an elephant or 20 people. Here the venom is 'milked' from the fangs of a live king cobra, a tiny amount is injected into horses in whose bodies antibodies are produced, and then extracted to make anti-venom serum. Cobra venom is also used to relieve pain and control cancer. King cobras are the only snakes that build a nest, piling up leaves and rotted vegetation and then laying up to 50 white, leathery eggs there. Fiercely aggressive when cornered, a king cobra will rise up, lifting about a third of its body off the ground, flaring out its hood with its false eyespots, hissing and growling as it moves forward to attack and spit venom.

Above: A snake charmer's music appears to spellbind several cobras.

Right: The beach at Chennai fairly bustles with vendors, fishermen attending their boats or nets, yoga practitioners, children building sand castles – and people playing games of cricket.

Andaman and Nicobar Islands

These 572 islands lie way across the Indian Ocean, 1000 miles (1600km) east of the mainland, and were once the haunt of pirates that preyed upon any merchant ships that strayed too near. The British colonized the islands in the 19th century and Christian missionaries inadvertently spread germs among the local tribes causing many deaths. Later a fearsome British prison was established at Port Blair. The islands eventually became Indian union territory (UT) in 1950 after Indian independence was declared in 1947.

Local tribes hunt pigs, fish, and turtles with harpoons made of metal. The Sentinelese and the Onges tribes still paint their naked bodies in the traditional way. Most of the 25,000 local people still live in grass huts in the forest, gathering nuts, roots, and honey, while 'newcomers' from India have also arrived to seek a new way of life. Hindus, Muslims, Christians, and Sikhs live together harmoniously and inter-religion marriages have led to an amazing racial and cultural mix. Historically, farming and fishing were the main revenue sources but increasing (albeit restricted) tourism is bringing some foreign income to Andaman.

The 2004 tsunami killed at least 7000 people on these islands. It caused great devastation when the 33ft (10m) wave followed in the wake of earthquake and aftershocks. People and their homes were swept away, with most of the victims taken completely by surprise. This impacted on an area where about

2200 varieties of plants have been recorded, 200 endemic and about 1300 not found in mainland India. Normally this plethora of species flourishes under a rich rainforest canopy or in forests, mangrove swamps, and bamboo stands. Ferns and orchids thrive under the evergreen tropical mantle as do some 50 kinds of mammal including wild boar, rodents, bats, barking and spotted deer, and feral elephants.

The air is busy with huge spectacular butterflies plus Andaman varieties of wood pigeon, hawk and scops owls. Shell life includes giant clams, green mussels, pearl and wing oysters, scallops, cockles, and chank. Huge, rare coconut crabs use their strong pincers to crack open coconuts and sometimes steal shiny items from houses – they are also called robber crabs as a result.

Above: *Coconut palms have strong adventitious roots that usually anchor them to the ground during hurricanes and typhoons.*

Opposite: *A candlelit vigil marks the anniversary of the tsunami as survivors remember the many lives lost when the great wave swept across the coastline of southern India and its offshore islands.*

Kolkata and its surroundings

Heading north toward Kolkata (formally known as Calcutta), you reach Chilka, a huge lagoon with an amazing mix of fresh, marine, and brackish waters, where one million migratory birds feed on some 225 species of fish. Often there are great flocks of flamingos plus gray and purple herons, egrets, spoonbills, storks, and white ibis. The narrow shifting lake and island shores are busy with snipes and sandpipers. Wagtails and lapwings haunt the mudflats and kingfishers and rollers are found in the trees. High above soar black and Brahimy kites, fishing eagles, white-bellied sea eagles, kestrels, and falcons. Rich fishing opportunities sustain the livelihoods of many human communities around the lagoon where fishermen catch prawn, crabs, and mackerel.

Above: Near to Kolkata are lagoons and lakes where storks (top), egrets (above), and vast flocks of flamingos (right) mingle with spoonbills, pelicans and ibis on some of the most important wetlands in the world.

Set in the Ganges delta and on the river Hooghly, Kolkata is the capital of West Bengal and enjoys a subtropical climate that is positively sweltering in the monsoon season. With an urban population of some 4.5 million, Kolkata is variously referred to as the cultural capital of India, the city of processions and the city of joy – its streets ever busy with rickshaws and taxis. This crowded place is home to Bengalis, Marwaris, Gujaratis, Punjabis, Parsis, Anglo-Indians, Jews, Armenians, and East Asians, a cosmopolitan mix that contributes to the energy and cultural richness of the city.

The British East India Company arrived here in pursuit of trade in 1690; in 1717 the Mughal emperor granted the Company freedom of trade in return for a yearly payment of 3000 rupees. The city was the scene of the infamous incident involving the Black Hole of Calcutta in 1756 when troops of the Nawab of Bengal supposedly held 146 British prisoners of war in a tiny dungeon. Most of them died and this incident became a cause célèbre of British imperial history. However, the total veracity of the account is now much debated. By 1772 Calcutta was the capital of British India and remained the nation's capital until supplanted by Delhi in 1911. The Indian Museum here is the oldest in Asia, established in 1814. There are many festivals and fairs in Kolkata including Diwali, the Hindu festival of lights that honors the victory of good over evil, when the streets glow with clay lamps and firecrackers.

Inland, the historic town of Bishnupur (Vishnupur) has wonderful brick temples – often distinguished by a tower mounted on a square, curved-roof building, modeled on thatch-roofed Bengali huts. This was once the site of a hugely important Hindu dynasty and is surrounded by old fortifications. It is also famous for its music and unique handicrafts, including silks and saris, conch-shell and bell-metal wares, plus the fabrication of sand terracotta toys, dolls, and horses. The most important festival here is Jhapan, which celebrates snake worship. Snake charmers perform, sometimes on decorated bullock carts and carriages, with king cobras, spectacled cobras, vipers, kraits, pythons, rat snakes, vine snakes, and flying snakes. Another colorful festival here is the Indra Puja when yellow turbans are presented to local chiefs.

Above and top: *Makar Sankranti is a one-day festival in mid-January marking the onset of the Sun's journey back to ascendancy in the northern hemisphere. Hindus worship the sun god on the river Hooghly bank while sadhus (ascetics) play traditional music. Monks and pilgrims take ceremonial cleansing bathes where the river Ganges meets the Bay of Bengal. Meanwhile, youngsters enjoy rice and sesame seed treats; many of them take the holy dip too, believing that they may then be blessed with fine-looking spouses in the future.*

Left: *The traffic in Kolkata is often disrupted by religious processions moving among the cars, buses, motorbikes, bicycles, rickshaws, yellow taxis with Bengal permits, and black-and-yellow (Kolkata city) cabs.*

Sundarbans

One of the largest delta regions and mangrove swamps in the world is found at the mouth of the Ganges that, with scant regard for political borders, flows into the ocean from both West Bengal and Bangladesh. It is called the Sundarbans. In this swampy delta terrain the thick jungle is slashed into an intricate crochet-pattern of mudflats and tiny islands criss-crossed by tidal waterways, rivers, small streams, and canals where saltwater and freshwater meet and the forest seems to float. The whole tract reaches inland for between 60 and 80 miles (100 and 130km). This unique ecosystem, a biosphere reserve and world heritage site, spreads over 54 islands and, lying just south of Kolkata, carries silt from the Himalayas through its maze of channels.

It is dominated by mangrove forests and derives its name from the upright Sundari trees that become rock hard when submerged for a long time. As a consequence they are used for house and shipbuilding, electric pylons, and railway sleepers. A good part of this forest is covered in water where fierce crocodiles swim and water monitors and river terrapins are found. Seagulls, geese, kingfishers, and white-bellied sea eagles soar above; monkeys, many snakes, and an estimated 30,000 spotted deer hide in the trees below. Looking just like fossil trilobites, there are also horseshoe or king crabs here; they have blue blood and their ten eyes can detect ultraviolet light.

This swamp is home to the endangered royal Bengal tiger (*Panthera tigris tigris*) that can reach a body length of up to 10ft (c.3m) long. It eats deer, boar, and fish stranded on the riverbeds at low tide. It also relishes rhesus macaque monkeys, antelopes, gaur (a type of ox), birds, lizards, turtles, frogs, and crabs. Leading a mainly solitary existence and hunting alone, less than 3000 Bengal tigers are left in the wild, with an estimated 400 to 600 living here – where they have a fearsome reputation as man-eaters. They kill between 100-250 people per year, usually attacking local dwellers who wor through the region on boats. In tribal folklore, Bonbibi, the goddess of the forest, is asked to protect local fishermen, wood-cutters, and honey-collectors (huge swarms of honeybees abound here) as 'The Tiger is always watching you.'

Above: White-bellied fish eagles eat fish, sea snakes, turtles, crabs, bats, and birds. They scavenge on garbage tips and around harbors and often harass smaller birds of prey until their catches are relinquished.

Right: Excellent swimmers, royal Bengal tigers love to cool off in the Sundarban waterways. They may also ambush animals drinking here or pursue other swimming prey.

Local sea creatures

Lurking in the waters here are Portuguese men-o'-war that immobilize prey using stinging cells in their long trailing tentacles as they pulsate in the silver waters around India's coastline. Sharks include the docile whale shark, the largest fish in the ocean at 50ft (15m) in length. It feeds only on plankton but is often killed to supply the shark-fin soup trade.

Long ago the dugong (*Dugong dugon*) gave rise to stories of mermaids, partly perhaps because of its mammary glands but also because this curious creature will sometimes rise vertically from the sea surface to breathe and look around, with floating sea grass clinging to its head like cascading hair. Sadly, since the 2004 tsunami, few have been spotted – possibly because of damage to the coral reefs where dugongs hide from predators like sharks.

Fish and crustaceans include bombay duck (a type of fish that is a familiar item on the Indian menu, usually served dried and salted), sardines, prawns, Neptune crabs, spiny lobsters (edible crayfish with long spiny antennae but no claws), rare oysters with precious pearls inside, and the conch – regarded as sacred and trumpeted during religious ceremonies or worship. The god Vishnu is believed to hold a conch representing the gift of life and, long ago, these beautiful shells were blown by warriors to announce battle.

Above: A Portuguese man-o'-war is not a single jellyfish but an iridescent colony of specialized life forms. Its venomous tentacles can administer extremely painful (and occasionally fatal) stings.

Opposite: A fishing boat on Goa's Palolem (or Paradise) beach, a beautiful crescent-shaped, white-sanded cove overlooking several small wooded islands – and a fine spot to watch dolphins.

Below: Sometimes the now endangered dugongs rise up and gaze around from the water, their mammary glands visible. This may have given rise to tales of mermaids or sirens but the allure of a mermaid's hypnotic beauty is not immediately apparent!

In conclusion

Traditional lifestyles struggle to survive today and the needs of India's fishing community sometimes clash with conservation regulations. Many marine habitats are – quite rightly – protected, but just as wildlife parks inland may compromise the needs of the farmer, so too some fishing communities feel threatened by conservation strictures. Such conflicts are never simple to resolve.

For instance, Jambudwip island in the Sundarbans was the subject of a dispute in 2002 when a fishing community that settles here each winter to dry fish was seen not only as a threat to the mangrove forests, but also to national security. The conflict ended in the government forces burning down the fishermen's huts and prohibiting them from landing on the island. Meanwhile, modern mechanized fishing off Kerala's shores threatens the livelihood of traditional fishermen, who have been fishing here for 2000 years and who traded with Arabs and Europeans many centuries ago. Traditions still

flourish happily in Kerala at the annual Onam festival, which is marked by feasts, boat races, singing, dancing, and wonderful colorful processions.

The growing presence of people along the coast, whether local communities or tourists, does threaten the future of sea turtles. All five species occur in India's seas and are legally protected, but many olive ridley sea turtles become trapped in large trawl-fishing nets and may be disturbed by bright lights on the busier parts of the coastline; hatchlings emerging from eggs buried in the sand on the beach at night are disoriented and head toward the lights rather than into the safety of the sea. Moreover, in Orissa, where mass nesting occurs, the coastline is eroding and often damaged by cyclonic storms.

Despite these problems, India's coastline remains a richly embroidered border embracing the nation's edges, famous for its sandy beaches, mangrove swamps, tidal sweeps and estuaries, fishing villages and glittering cities – all home to a plethora of sea life and colorful local traditions.

LIFE IN THE FORESTS

India has so many different types of forest – tropical, subtropical, monsoon, semi-evergreen rainforests, and temperate woodlands. Some forests are composed of short thorny trees and shrubs; some are home to glorious pine trees; some have gorgeous orchids gleaming in the gloom. The woodland may cling to mountainsides, grow to the edge of deserts or wrap around the coast. There are gushing waterfalls and streams amid the greenery and mighty rivers cruising along beneath the trees. Among the many creatures hiding here are tigers, leopards, golden and marbled cats, gibbons, lorises, macaques, snakes, and countless leaping monkeys.

LIFE IN THE FORESTS

Many of the great tracts of India's forests are ancient woodlands; they have evolved over centuries to produce a rich habitat, bustling with insects scurrying through the thick plant cover and home to the most magnificent wildlife including endangered tigers, intelligent elephants, sleek leopards, cheeky macaques, and sinuous pythons. This is an environment that has long been revered by its human dwellers, with sacred groves being the site for ancient religious ceremonies involving trees and plants. Sadly, India's increasing population today encroaches on much of the jungle and the extent of its green mantle is diminishing, while the depredations of hunting have also taken their toll on forest creatures.

Above: A jungle babbler in Keoladeo Ghana National Park, Rajasthan. This noisy forest bird chatters to others in the flock, making mewing calls, chirps, and squeaks. It conceals its nests in dense foliage.

Right: Eucalyptus trees are quick growers, many reaching a great height. These tall slender specimens are in the Nilgiri Hills.

Many types of forest

While the tropical and subtropical forests may initially seize the imagination and command our attention, the splendid panorama of India's forests also includes semi-evergreen rainforests, moist deciduous monsoon forests, thorn forests, subtropical pine forests, temperate montane forests (that grow on mountains above 3000ft), riparian forests (that grow adjacent to water) and associated swamps and grasslands. There are forests in the Himalayas as well as tropical rainforests that hug the equatorial belt, with deciduous forests in central and southern areas and moist deciduous forests in the east.

The term jungle implies a dense, hot, humid forest with thickets of tropical shrubs and trees entwined with vines. India has many such steamy environments, including the evergreen tropical rainforests in the Western Ghats that fringe the Arabian Sea coastline of peninsular India, the rainforests in the greater Assam region in the northeast and western Bengal, and those on the Andaman and Nicobar Islands. These are rich burgeoning environments, lushly green, that hum with the spirit of life.

In fact, tropical rainforest sweeps across much of the mainland. Heavy rainfall beats down, encouraging some 200 species of trees to flourish. In its hot central zone are the giants – tall light-seeking trees that rise to the upper story of the forest canopy to spread their foliage in the sunlight. Their crowns create a dense, light-blocking canopy that may be some 23ft (7m)- deep. Down below is a warm and humid world where no winds penetrate and the dense shade creates a moist steamy environment. Here shorter trees form the middle story where monkeys and squirrels scamper, while a myriad creatures and plants inhabit the lower ground levels. Plants have adapted to survive below the ceiling canopy, some with leaves that can swivel to maximize their light intake and jointed at the base of the stalk so that they can follow the Sun as the world spins.

The many different types of forest in India are the haunt of tigers and leopards, as well as lesser feline species like golden and marbled cats. Primates include gibbons, slow lorises, stumptailed macaques, and langur monkeys. Buffalo and elephants roam the hills; squirrels, porcupines, civets, mongooses, and shrews scurry among the trees where pythons glide. Countless herbs and medicinal plants thrive. Arunachal Pradesh boasts over five hundred varieties of orchids, many rare or endangered – and two that, legend has it, decked the epic heroines Sita and Draupadi and so are called *Sita-Pushpa* and *Draupadi Pushpa*.

Above: Thick tree cover in Periyar National Park, a verdant stretch of forest in Kerala.

Opposite: A wary golden cat stares ahead from the shelter of the dense forest. Asian folklore claims that a single hair from the golden cat will protect you from tigers.

Above: An elephant quenches its thirst at the edge of the river, its reflection rippling below. Most elephants seem to recognize that a reflection is their own image, which scientists consider a mark of a superior intelligence.

Opposite: Spotted deer are nervous and alert. They often forage for titbits dropped by langurs munching in the trees above and also appreciate the langurs' early-warning calls when danger approaches.

Rainforests boast an enormous number of tree species. Here, shooting up from the decaying vegetation, are mighty woody liana vines that embrace and scramble up tall tree trunks. Air plants (or epiphytes – plants that grow upon other living plants) include the brilliant bromeliads that, despite being rootless, seem to flourish miraculously, able to absorb nutrients and moisture from the air and thus survive in the hollows of trees or clinging to branches. At the edges of the rainforest – or where the trees are interrupted by rivers – a little more light penetrates: these are true jungle areas where plant life can run riot in the sunlight and clumps of bamboo thrive along stream edges.

Elephants, Indian bison, rhinoceroses, and tigers live mainly in wet forested regions. There are monsoon forests too that can be categorized as dry forests or tropical deciduous forests. Here hardwood sal trees dominate; this is said to be the tree under which Buddha was born and so it is worshiped by Buddhists and Hindus in India. Its sturdy timber is used for railway sleepers, house timbers, bridge building, and the construction of wheels; its resin serves as incense and for caulking boats; its seeds are a source of fat and sal seed cake is fed to poultry and pigs; its fruit oil is burned in earthen lamps and, during a famine, the fruit may be ground into flour.

In a tropical deciduous forest, there are more open areas of woodland, although the atmosphere is still hot and humid, and here the trees are not evergreen giants. Instead they lose their leaves, generally shedding their foliage during the dry season and then breaking into leaf again when the next rainy season comes.

There are also forests around the mangrove swamps that stretch inland from the coasts. Here spotted deer and wild boar trot between the trees while rhesus monkeys swing through the trees above. The waters and banks are busy with mighty saltwater crocodiles, countless scampering crabs – and water monitors, huge muscular lizards. Some specimens may reach nearly 10ft (3m) in length.

Here too mud skippers are found, fish that can swim and also skip across on dry land; some even climb trees, using their fins as suckers and graspers while breathing from an expanded gill chamber that acts like a scuba diver's oxygen cylinder. Atop its head, its fast-moving eyes enable it to see both under and above the water. Up above in the trees, weaver ants build nests in a most unusual way – they hold ant larvae in their jaws and then use strands of silk from the larva's salivary glands to sew large leaves together.

Above: The Sundarbans has the world's largest mangrove forest. Swamps hug the edges of both land and sea; brackish and saline tidal waters meet as roots protect coasts from erosion and create perfect habitats for creatures like fiddler crabs.

Conservation efforts

Conservation came early to India's forests, although the initial stimulus was human – rather than wildlife – needs. Between 1865 and 1894 reserves were established to satisfy imperial desires for more forest to serve as hunting grounds and to ensure these remained sustainable. From 1926 to 1947, large-scale afforestation on bare or cultivated land in the Punjab and Uttar Pradesh served to increase hunting areas. By the early 1930s, the conservation of wildlife became a pressing issue and many Indian rulers began to direct efforts to conserve habitats and many of the creatures therein. While the motives of these conservationist hunters (who managed, meantime, to kill at least 5000 tigers) were not entirely altruistic, the preservation of habitats may, nevertheless, have helped to save the tigers from complete extinction. These protected areas would later form the basis for today's national parks.

Above: Young sambar deer usually stay well hidden in thick vegetation. They become fully independent of their parents at about one year old. They live in damp woodland environments, usually close to marshes or swamps, and may be preyed upon by tigers.

Himalayan forests and tigers

In the western Himalayas, temperate deciduous forests mark the lower elevations while coniferous forests flourish above, until the tree line vanishes at higher altitudes. The eastern Himalayas have extensive deciduous forest cover while in northeastern India, close to Bangladesh, there is tropical evergreen forest in the wet lowlands and temperate deciduous forest in drier, cooler areas. Below the timber line, the Great Himalayas encompass valuable forests of fir, spruce, juniper, cypress, and birch.

Many leopards, rhinoceroses, and deer once inhabited the forested sub-Himalayan foothills but, just as in many other parts of the world, there are growing fears that the present level of deforestation threatens many creatures that depend on the tree cover. In the Indian Himalayas, particularly its western regions, tigers, black bears, musk deer, leopards, golden eagles, and bearded vultures are at risk. The subtropical and temperate forests are home to the endangered Hoolock gibbon and the Himalayan tahr (a close relative of the wild goat) that already face severe habitat loss.

Efforts are being made to save these creatures. Tucked away in the northernmost state of Arunachal Pradesh is the Namdhapa National Park, which is famous for the extremely elusive snow and clouded leopards. The park is also a tiger reserve.

The Corbett Tiger reserve lies in the foothills of the Himalayas in the state of Uttaranchal. This was India's first national park and is now a renowned tiger reserve. It is named after Jim Corbett, a famous hunter turned conservationist. Some 580 species of resident and migratory birds have been recorded in and around the reserve, as well as 49 diurnal raptor species. This is a great place to spot great pied hornbills, fishing eagles, brown hawk-owls, great hornbills, kingfishers, brown dippers, redstarts, forktails and the blue-bearded bee-eater.

The park retains an awesome majesty and the sense of a world that is both inspiring and dangerous. This is the kind of primal jungle that inspired Rudyard Kipling and his *Jungle Book* stories, not least in his portrayal of tigers.

Above and opposite: Subtropical broadleaf forests grow in the Himalayan foothills, with temperate broadleaf woodlands higher up, and conifers the last to cling to rising peaks.

Vanishing tigers

Tigers (*Panthera tigris*) are one of the most endangered species on the planet and the Bali, Javan, and Caspian tigers are already extinct. Once upon a time there were about a 100,000 tigers in the wild and India alone boasted over 40,000 tigers in the early 1900s. Regrettably numbers have since been reduced by at least 95 percent. A survey published in May 2007 suggests that only 1200, or even fewer, may survive in the wild today. Ranthambore National Park has seen an increase in poaching and has only 32 tigers left, while in Madhya Pradesh in central India, once a tiger stronghold, numbers have crashed from an estimated 700 to only 265. In the Jim Corbett Tiger Reserve the population is relatively stable at about 112.

So this magnificent creature is now highly endangered. Poachers have killed countless tigers to sell their precious skins (each with a unique pattern of stripes), to turn tiger claws and whiskers into aphrodisiacs and rheumatism cures, and sell ground-up tiger bones as a supposed healing potion. The devoted mother tigress is very protective of her cubs, caring for them until they are about two and a half years old. Nonetheless, only half the cubs born survive to reach maturity and, of these, only 40 percent will establish territory and sire their own offspring. Loss of habitat takes a heavy toll too.

The national animal of India, this powerful agile hunter inhabits a variety of forests – moist monsoon, riparian, tropical dry, and tropical evergreen broadleaf. It needs good cover, water, and abundant prey. Tigers hunt alone, taking advantage of their great size and strength – they are the largest members of the cat family at over 10 to 11ft (3m) from head to tail with males weighing up to 570lb (258kg). Fearsome sharp teeth, incredibly strong jaws, and formidable retractile claws help them kill prey such as antelope, deer, wild pigs, and goats, with an occasional lizard, bird, turtle, fish, crab, or frog to supplement the diet – unless a determined hyena or jackal drives the tiger away from its kill.

During hot daylight hours, tigers rest in the shade and then wake to prowl the jungle between dusk and dawn. They remain aware of other tigers through their scent and scratch marks as they stalk their prey, helped by their keen eyesight and sharp hearing. They are excellent swimmers too and love to keep cool in water. Most tigers bear the familiar orange-brown coat with black stripes, but occasionally a white one may be born – or the rare golden tabby with a white coat, golden patches, and pale stripes.

There are also small remnants of rainforest with numerous waterfalls in the state of Orissa where the Simlipal National Park in the northern forested belt was established as one of the earliest tiger reserves. It is set in lush grassland and sal forests, and was declared a sanctuary in 1979. Some 82 species of orchids and 231 bird species have been identified here.

Above left: A tigress will fiercely defend her young cubs.

Above right: In Bandhavgarh National Park there are stands of sal and bamboo with mixed forests in the higher hills. These visitors observe one of the resident tigers from the safe vantage point of an elephant.

Opposite: No wild white tigers have been reported in the last 50 years and less than 12 were in the previous 50. All were in Bandhavgarh where the renowned white tiger cub, Mohan, was captured in 1951.

Following pages: The tiger is an awe-inspiring and powerful animal.

Northwest India and the Gir Forest

This is largely an arid area with the state of Rajasthan being dominated by the Thar Desert, which stretches into Pakistan. However, Sariska Wildlife Sanctuary is one of the few forest pockets in the Aravalli range of mountains in Rajasthan. The sanctuary consists of dry deciduous forest that turns lush and green only during the monsoons. It is home to more than 200 bird species, including crested serpent eagles, gray hornbills, golden orioles, great gray shrikes, and tailor birds.

Leopards (*Panthera pardus*) live here too, their bright sleek coats marked with small, close-set, black rosettes. Leopard fur grows quite long and dense in colder regions but is shorter and smoother in tropical zones. When these shy, elusive creatures are confronted and need to defend themselves, they will stretch their backs, stick out their shoulder blades, and lower their heads as a warning to any potential aggressor. Leopards are also found in Ranthambore National Park in Rajasthan.

The Gir Forest, which lies farther south in Gujarat, enjoys a tropical monsoon climate but it can be dry when the summer heat peaks above a landscape where more than 400 plant species grow. The Gir has open scrub country, dry deciduous and tropical thorn forest, hot sulfur springs, deep ravines, steep rocky hills and with an evergreen corridor running along the sides of the many rivers, and streams where mixed deciduous trees include lots of teak plus acacia, banyan, jamun, tendu, and dhak. The Gir is the largest dry deciduous forest in western India. It is an important biological research and scientific area of great value.

About 7000 Maldharis lead a nomadic lifestyle here in 50 or so scattered settlements, rearing cattle, selling dairy products, and

depending on the forest for fuel. The constant grazing of their numerous cattle threatens the survival of the vegetation.

The brown fish owl catches fish and frogs. It has no feathers to get wet on its lower legs and so can cleanly snatch up prey from the surface of the water with its feet – its grip on the slippery fish made more secure by spiny scales on the soles of its talons.

Of all the protected areas in India, Gir has the highest population of the wide-snouted marsh (or mugger) crocodiles (*Crocodylus palustris*). During a very hot dry season, these reptiles may migrate great distances over land in search of water and dig burrows in which to shelter. Marsh crocodiles eat fish, reptiles and mammals – often dragging prey into the water to drown it. Their name comes from the Hindi word *magar* meaning 'water monster.'

Above: Banyan trees, sometimes called strangler figs, scramble up host trees and send down aerial roots that can develop into huge trunks.

Above left: The diet of sambar deer (seen here in Ranthambore National Park) includes grass, herbs, sprigs of plants, and fruit.

Opposite: Teak is found mainly in the eastern half of the Gir forest.

Cats in the wild

The cats here include about 500 leopards, jungle cats, Indian desert cats, and the rare rusty-spotted cats but the area is famous as the only place in the world where Asiatic lions roam, some 350 prowling the hilly terrain and forests. Protected since the early 1900s, they are smaller than their African counterparts at 8 to 10ft (2.5 to 2.9m) in length.

The Asiatic lion (*Panthera leo persica*) once ranged from northwest India through Persia to Arabia but it became a coveted trophy item and was over-hunted during the British Raj era. Now it is rated as one of the most endangered large carnivores. Sadly, many lions have met a sorry end by falling into open wells dug by the Maldharis – either drowning as a result or being unable to escape because of bones broken in the fall. Electric fences erected to keep them from livestock have also claimed many victims and some lions have been deliberately poisoned for attacking livestock.

Asiatic lions live in prides and communicate by grunts, miaows, growls, moans, and roars. They prey on sambar, chital, nilgai, wild pigs, deer (and occasionally on goats) but may succumb to a leopard attack.

Above: Outside Africa, Gir is the only place where lions roam wild. Only a century ago the Asiatic lion was threatened with extinction. Less than 20 survived in 1913 but a shooting ban allowed their numbers to recover.

Left: Leopards are accomplished stalkers, strong swimmers, and agile climbers who can descend from a tree headfirst.

Life in the northeastern forests

On the peninsular uplands, deciduous monsoon and scrub forests wrap their green mantle around the slopes. In the forests in the greater Assam region in the northeast and the Assam Valley the giant *Dipterocarpus macrocarpus* and *Shorea assamica* trees grow, occasionally reaching an impressive girth of up to 23ft (7m) and a height of 165ft (50m). The monsoon forests are full of moist sal (*Shorea robusta*) trees. High humidity encourages a rich variety of superb orchids to flourish.

The Hoolock gibbon (*Bunopithecus hoolock*), south Asia's only ape, swings through the branches on sinuous long arms as it searches for fruits, insects, and sweet leaves to eat. The black males have impressive white brows; females are gray-brown but,

remarkably, their babies sport milky white fur for some six months or so. The strong family group maintains a defined territory by making frequent loud calls and songs.

The valley provides one of the last wild habitats for Asian elephants (*Elephas maximus*). Although slightly smaller than their African counterparts, these elephants are still one of the largest land mammals on Earth, standing up to 10ft (3m) tall at the shoulder. They have played a vital part in Indian culture for thousands of years, and have been used for forestry work, to move heavy objects, as load-bearers and for transportation. In this part of India, however, the elephants are wild and they constantly march through the trees in search of grass, bark, leaves, shoots and roots, bamboo, creepers, and seasonal fruits to satisfy their prodigious appetites.

Related females and young elephants live in a matriarchal family herd of eight to 100 individuals. Adult males often stay close to the herds with other males, or wander farther afield as solitary animals but they are rarely out of touch with one another. Elephants communicate through low-frequency sounds, high-pitched calls and loud trumpeting.

The Assam Valley is the largest tea-growing area in the world: over 600 tea estates produce rich, full-bodied tea with a distinctive malty taste. Here festivals known as bihus mark the seasons and the farming cycle at three times of the year – Rongali bihu to mark spring's arrival, sowing seed, and the bathing of cows in local rivers or ponds; Kongali bihu when the fields are lush but the barns are still empty; and Bhogali bihu, a harvest thanksgiving when crops fill the barns.

Above: *Women at work in an Assam tea plantation – India is the world's largest tea producer, with some 55 percent of its 944,000 US ton (856 million kilogram) output being produced in Assam.*

Opposite: *Adult and baby Asian elephants march along at the edge of the forest. At puberty, female elephants will remain with their mothers as part of the herd, while males leave the family, usually joining bull groups but sometimes remaining solitary.*

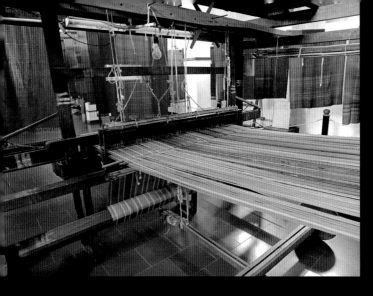

These pages: The Assam valley is a place of great vibrancy and color, where the many ethnic groups and cultures revel in creating rich fabrics including soft silks, beautifully embroidered garments, and lavish jewelry – as well as musical instruments, cane and bamboo products, items in bell metal and brass, toys, masks, and pottery.

Above: A young woman harvests coffee beans that have been produced in the state of Karnataka for over a hundred years and today represent 70 percent of India's shade-grown coffee crop.

Opposite above: The sambar stag has sturdy tall antlers – that may exceed 40in (100cm) in height – with forked tips.

Opposite below: India is a major producer of rubber; sometimes the dripping latex is collected in coconut shells.

The Western Ghats and Goa

The Western Ghats mountains of Maharashtra spread from the Satpura Range to the north, and continue south past Goa to the state of Karnataka, fringing the Arabian Sea coastline of peninsular India. Monsoon forests occur both on the coastal fringes of the Ghats and on the eastern side where there is less rainfall. On the wetter slopes, deciduous tropical monsoon forest and evergreen cover flourish. The Western Ghats are rich in the production of cash crops and spices including coffee, cocoa, cardamom, rubber, tea, and pepper.

Beyond the coastal fringe are many forest-clad slopes in Goa and the Western Ghats where the rich wildlife includes a type of ox called gaur (*Bos gaurus*). These are dark brown wild cattle with lighter lower limbs that resemble legs dressed in white or tan socks. Given a choice, gaur eat grass but they will consume leaves and creepers too. Only about 1000 gaur remain in the wild.

Here too are grazing packs of large dark brown sambar (*Cervus unicolor*), a type of maned Asian deer, while the trees provide cover for spotted deer, leopards, and panthers, elephants, Malayan giant squirrels, pythons, and cobras. A keen eye might also seek out wild boar, porcupines, scaly anteaters, and the diminutive flying lizard gliding down from the treetops.

Plants and trees in the Goa area include evergreens and canes, rosewood, the fascinatingly named naked maiden of the forest, thorny bamboo, and giant entwining lianas. Here the air throngs with slate birds (or ruby throated yellow bulbuls), golden-backed woodpeckers, and the common gray hornbill.

At the Cotigao wildlife sanctuary in Goa tall trees dominate the forests so that scant light reaches the ground and moist-deciduous vegetation is interspersed with semi-evergreen and evergreen patches. Among these dense forests, where gushing streams and waterfalls froth with silver bubbles, lurk shy gazelles, sloth bears, porcupines, panthers, monkeys, hyenas, gaur, and boar.

The Western Ghats and forests flow on through Kerala where Indian rosewood (*Dalbergia latifolia*) grows beside tall teak trees and the Indian kino tree (*Pterocarpus marsupium*), also known as the Malabar kino. This has long been used in Ayurvedic medicine to cure diabetes and other ills, and also to relieve inflammation, coughs and toothache, as an astringent, and to darken gray hair. Sadly there has been some organized smuggling of valuable timbers, such as teak, rosewood, and sandalwood,

while local dependency on forest resources inevitably leads to deforestation. These fragile areas of tree cover, with epiphytic orchids, mosses, and ferns, are now threatened.

Bullfrogs flaunt their huge vocal sacs during their monsoon mating season here, while hoping to escape the attentions of spectacled and king cobras. Great shaggy sloth bears (*Melursus ursinus*) may seek a treasure of succulent insects in the termite mounds, their curved ivory claws being well adapted for digging and delving, as elephants crash their way through an interior that hides spotted deer, majestic muntjac stags, tall sambar deer, and gaur that graze at dusk, followed by swirling clouds of mosquitoes. The untidy-looking sloth bear is a nocturnal browser here, and is characterized by its unkempt hair and long sharp claws.

Cats include growling tigers and lithe, beautifully spotted leopards (*Panthera pardus*) – these graceful, agile climbers can slither down trees head-first. They are generally nocturnal and solitary, moving stealthily as they stalk the thick forests and rocky outcrops. These are secretive creatures that remain hidden from all but the most expert eyes, with often only the twitch of a dangling tail to hint at their presence. Leopards often store a larger kill up in a tree to eat later, safe from the intrusion of thieving hyenas or lions. Black (melanistic) leopards are not uncommon in the Ghats and eastern India.

Toddy cats (*Paradoxurus hermaphroditus*) are civets with thickly furred tails, small ears, and pointed snouts. Nocturnal prowlers, they are named for their habit of stealing juice from vessels placed in palm trees to collect the sap to make into toddy or palm sugar. Bonnet macaque monkeys (*Macaca radiata*) inhabit wet lowland and dry deciduous forest and are also aptly named after the furry cap of hair that swirls out from the center of the head.

Some tribal villages are found in this part of India and various customary ways of life continue, but this is a changing world as forests are heavily logged or converted to plantations for tea, coffee, rubber, palm oil, teak, eucalyptus, and wattle. Grazing cattle and goats and forest fires add to erosion problems and as people farm ever closer to protected wildlife areas, they resent raiding elephants damaging their crops and leopards killing their livestock.

Traditional food here often features a profusion of vegetarian items served on banana leaves, while Parsi cuisine combines Persian and Indian cooking, using mint, coriander, cumin, and ginger. Living as they do next to coconut plantations, locals often quench their thirst with coconut juice.

Above: *The black panther, like all leopards, is a highly secretive, solitary cat, usually hunting at night or very early in the morning and remaining well hidden during daylight hours.*

Opposite left: *Forest fires are a major threat in the Western Ghats, an area of great biodiversity.*

Above right: *Nut palm trees include the betel. The grated nut is often chewed here, sometimes with tobacco or flavored with spices, and it may be offered to guests.*

Right: *A gaur bull is the largest and most powerful of all the world's wild cattle, sometimes reaching a shoulder height of around 6-7ft (2m).*

These pages: Local markets offer a vast range of colorful Indian spices
(masala is the Hindi word for spice), usually grown in one of the millions
of tiny holdings that are a vital source of livelihood in rural areas. The
spice trade inspired many voyages of exploration in the past and
brought great wealth and power to merchants in cities such as Venice

The Silent Valley, Kerala

This national park is one of many patches of dense evergreen forest in the south that provides shelter for a variety of wildlife including elephants, gaur (Indian bison), pine martens, and otters. Here, within the mountain folds of the Nilgiris district, enclosed by a ring of hills, lie deep wooded ravines, rushing waters, gorges, and unspoiled subtropical and tropical moist evergreen forests where over 100 plant species are the source of vital Ayurvedic medicine ingredients. There are many tall teak trees; about a dozen people can squeeze into the hollow trunk of one huge Kattualying specimen here. Rare orchids bloom and spices include cardamon and black pepper.

Some of the indigenous Mudugar and Irula tribespeople now work as forest rangers and guides here – often rolling up their trouser legs so that they can quickly spot and remove the forest leeches clinging to their skin, ever-ready to bloat on blood as the guides maneuver through a remote habitat where many of India's most splendid animals live. There are elephants, tigers, leopards, fishing cats, gaur, civets, sloth bears, flying squirrels, lion-tailed macaques, mongooses, clawless otters, and the Indian pangolin or scaly anteater (*Manis crassicaudata*). This creature is protected by its scaly armor and has a long agile tongue with muscular attachments reaching all the way to its pelvis. Here too are Malabar giant squirrels, Nilgiri langur, and various types of deer. Wild dogs roam, hairy-winged and fruit bats dangle from the trees, various amphibians, lizard species and snakes, including nest-building king cobras, each fill their particular slot in the ecological spectrum.

About 100 butterfly and 400 moth species flutter their vibrantly colored (and often enormous) wings in-between trees where bird

species include Malabar parakeets, Malabar laughing thrushes, Nilgiri wood-pigeons, gray-headed bulbuls, and the fruit-eating great Indian hornbill, which has an enormous wingspan. Male hornbills build nests in hollow tree trunks and then bizarrely

lock their life-long partners safely inside behind seals made from wood bark, dirt, and their droppings. Here the females stay for up to three months, as the males feed them, and then the young, via a slit in the prison door.

Above and opposite: *Indian smooth-coated otters live in the mangrove forests, enjoying a diet that consists mainly of fish but also includes the shrimps, crayfish, crabs, mudskippers, frogs, birds, rats, and insects that inhabit this marginal world.*

Chinnar Wildlife Sanctuary

Set in the rain shadow of Kerala's Western Ghats, with its fine Marayoor sandal forest and beautiful Thoovanam waterfalls is Chinnar Wildlife Sanctuary. Thorny scrub and dry deciduous forests populate a rippling landscape punctuated by craggy rocks. This varied habitat is home to many creatures including tigers, elephants, bonnet macaques and Hanuman monkeys, rabbits, gaur, sambar and spotted deer, plus turtles, kraits, vipers, and spectacled cobras. It is one of only two places where India's endangered giant grizzled squirrel lives.

Birds include little cormorants, darters, black eagles, and the exotic Indian peacock (*Pavo cristatus*). This is the national bird of India and is generally found in jungle areas close to water, from south of the Himalayas to India's southern tip. It has a distinctive crest, long, slender neck and an ornamental train that may be 64in (1.6m) long, accounting for 60 percent of its total body length. Each of the magnificent blue-green tail feathers has an ornamental eye-spot and, when displaying to a female, the peacock erects these into a spectacular shuddering fan shot with iridescent hues that shimmer and change in the varying light.

Phoenician traders in the time of King Solomon (c.1000 BC) presented these fine birds to the Egyptian pharaohs and introduced them into present-day Syria. Legends claim that the peafowl can charm snakes and addle their eggs. The birds feature in a good deal of folklore and mythology and are considered sacred by Hindus. The god Kartikeya (Lord Karthikeyan – son of Lord Shiva and Parvati [or Shakti] and brother of the god Ganesh) rides on the back of a peacock, while the image of Indra, the god of thunder, rains, and war, was depicted as a peacock into which he had transformed to escape a demon.

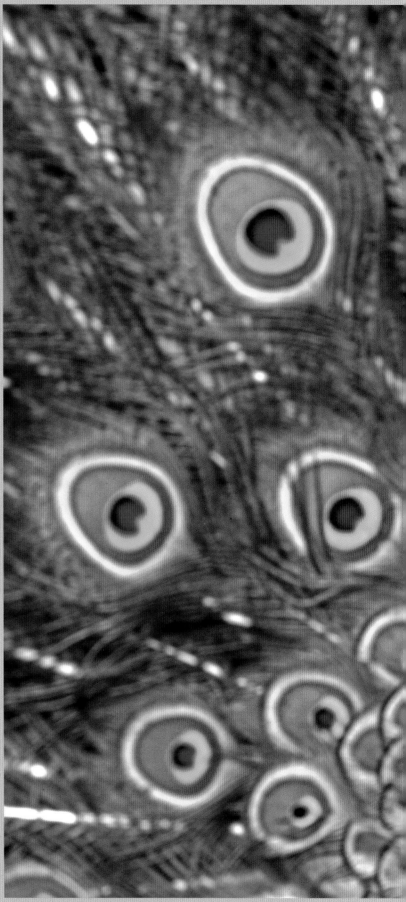

Despite this religious significance, the peacock population is fast dwindling through habitat loss, the indiscriminate use of pesticides, and the actions of poachers who, with scant regard for the peacock's history, trade in their fine feathers.

Above and opposite: *India's national bird, the magnificent peacock,*
roosts in trees but forages and nests on the ground near watering holes.
Its distinctive haunting cries ring out wherever it is found. It is said that
King Solomon adored these gorgeous birds.

Forest snakes

The spectacled or Indian cobra (*Naja naja*) is found throughout mainland India. It is the one most often used by snake charmers – probably because of the way it seems to sway to the rhythm of a flute as it follows the movement of the pipe and senses vibrations from the music and the tapping of the snake charmer's foot. Its raised threat posture adds to the drama. As well as its lethal bite, the Indian cobra may spit venom into an opponent's eyes, ejecting this through its fangs in twin jets that can shoot across a distance of at least 6.5ft (2m). The king cobra (*Ophiophagus hannah*) is also highly venomous. It feeds on rodents, lizards, and frogs and is found in many forested areas.

The cobra appears in Hindu mythology as a powerful deity and at the Serpent Festival (Naga panchami), held after the monsoon rains, snake effigies may be anointed and worshiped, while live cobras are often brought into the villages and fed. This Hindu festival is observed partly to guard against the danger of snakebites in the monsoon months.

There are over 270 species of snakes in India, of which about 60 are venomous. The handsome golden tree snake (*Chrysopelea ornata*) has an extraordinary power of flight – it glides through tall trees, spreading its ribs to form a concave underside to provide some aerodynamic lift. It rests and hides among dense foliage but, if threatened by a bird of prey or climbing mammal, it can launch itself into the air to escape from the branches. The paradise tree snake (*Chrysopelea paradisi*), whose favorite haunt is the crown of coconut palms, can also fly and seems to glide through the air from tree to tree, its brilliant fluorescent green helping its camouflage among the foliage once it lands. It is more easily spotted when sunning itself at the forest edge.

Above left: *The paradise tree snake glides between coconut palms by launching itself into the air and flattening its body.*

Above right: *Often used by snake charmers, the Indian cobra makes a dramatic threat display as it rises up, spreading its hood. Its bite can be fatal in less than an hour.*

Andaman and Nicobar rainforests

The Andaman and Nicobar islands have tropical evergreen and semi-evergreen rainforests as well as tropical moist monsoon forests. The canopied evergreen rainforests of the islands are home to some 3000 species of plants including mangroves, epiphytes, 130 types of fern, 100 orchid species, palms, woody climbers, gujan trees, and a wide variety of tropical fruits. Trees include teak, mahogany, and the giant Andaman redwood. Many elephants were brought here to serve the timber industry.

Twelve aboriginal tribes once lived in this area but their populations were decimated by European diseases introduced by travelers and by loss of land. From a pool of about 5000 local people, only some 400 remain. The understandably hostile Sentinelese, who inhabit North Sentinel Island, may still warn off strangers with arrow fire. Nicobar tribes include Nicobarese and Shompen peoples while Negrito tribes include Jarawas (traditional hunter-gatherers), Great Andamanese, Onges, and the fierce Sentinelese.

Local birdlife includes great black woodpeckers and green imperial pigeons, sunbirds, kingfishers, and eagles. The Andaman islands are home to 445 reptile species, 13 of which are endemic. Of the 12 amphibian species here, seven are endemic. All are frogs and toads, many of which fall victim to tree snakes that assume a green hue here in order to hide from the sharp eyes of the Andaman serpent-eagle.

Above: The 572 Andaman and Nicobar islands, formed by a submarine mountain range, support rich ecosystems.

Following pages, left: This Nicobar pigeon has superb, iridescent green and blue plumage. Flocks fly from one small wooded island to another, feeding on the forest floor.

Following pages, right: White-throated kingfishers catch fish, tadpoles, grasshoppers, crabs, frogs, beetles, lizards, centipedes, and scorpions. They beat venomous prey against a perch to remove their stings and can even catch swarming termites in mid-flight.

Primates of the forest

Swinging through the trees in India's forest belts are many bright-eyed monkeys, langurs, and gibbons. Monkeys have a reputation for being mischievous and, indeed, when they encroach on human settlements they will take any opportunity to steal food, especially juicy fruits. A group of macaques, for example, may well run amok in a market or raid a kitchen. Monkeys are not immune to the attractions of alcohol either, and they have even been reported as stealing from pots of fermenting marijuana leaves being prepared as part of a New Year offering to Hindu gods. Apparently they became very aggressive after quaffing the intoxicating brew.

Rather more reserved creatures include the slow loris found creeping through the trees in Assam and the saucer-eyed slender loris that lives in many parts of southern India. The slender loris (*Loris tardigradus*) is a small, nocturnal primate with huge, saucer-like eyes that is found in the tropical rainforests of southern India. It hides from predators in thick, thorny vegetation where its long fingers seize passing insects. Rhesus macaques enjoy nibbling insects too, adding termites, grasshoppers, ants, and beetles to an all-embracing diet of eggs, fruit, flowers, buds, leaves, seeds, grass, clover, roots, bark, mushrooms, fish, and shellfish.

Above: The lion-tailed macaque lives in the evergreen broadleaf forests of India's southwest hill country. Its face is framed by a long brown-gray mane and the tail has a distinctive tuft.

Right: Rhesus macaques are opportunistic foragers, enjoying all the succulent items of food that a tropical or dry deciduous forest offers.

Common or Hanuman langurs (*Presbytis entellus*) are found throughout the nation, with the Nilgiri langur at home in the Western Ghats and surrounding hills. Langurs are easygoing creatures – lanky and long-tailed with bushy eyebrows, chin tufts and crests of hair atop their heads. They inhabit humid forests, woodlands, and mangrove swamps – and sometimes even visit temples, as Hindus worship these animals and tempt them with titbits here. The very rare and beautiful golden langur (*Trachypithecus geei*) was discovered by – and named for – the renowned naturalist E.P. Gee in 1955. It has a black, hairless face and a long, pale beard that seems to have a golden iridescence in bright sunlight. Its leaps through the trees in dense deciduous tropical forests in northwestern Assam, south-central Bhutan, and on both banks of the Brahmaputra river.

Macaques include the pig-tailed macaque in the Naga Hills, the rhesus macaque in Himalayan regions and northern India, and bonnet macaques in the Indian peninsula from Mumbai in the west to Godavari in the east. The lion-tailed macaque (*Macaca silenus*) lives in dense, wet forests in the Western Ghats from Kanara to Kerala where it spends most of its time high up in the trees. Its bold black and white face markings improve its camouflage in dappled sunlight. This handsome creature is named after its long tail with a tasseled end – just like that of a lion. These shy creatures are excellent swimmers.

Hoolock gibbons swing languorously through the trees in the Garo and Khasi hills in Meghalaya state and in the forests of Assam and Manipur. They live in small family groups and spend a good deal of time finding tasty fruit to eat, as well as leaves, flowers, buds, and a few insects and spiders. When the sun proves too hot for activity in the trees, they retire to rest in lower shadier spots.

In 2004, in the state of Arunachal Pradesh, in the rugged mountains and extensive forest cover of the remote northeast, researchers discovered a new species of monkey, the Arunachal macaque (*Macaca munzala*), a large brown primate with a relatively short tail. The first new monkey species named in over a century, it was known to locals long before and lives in remote areas above 6500ft (2000m). It is highly endangered.

Opposite: The adult male Hoolock gibbon is black but with prominent white eyebrows. His monogamous female partner is gold or brownish buff, while the babies have milky white fur.

Above: Here a trio of Hanuman langurs sit in formation on a branch, but in fact they spend up to 80 percent of their time on the ground, searching for fallen fruit, nuts, seeds, and fungi.

Roads bring change

Forests are essentially busy habitats full of all manner of creatures from small scurrying rodents, bustling squirrels, and porcupines, to elegant deer and regal tigers. However, much is changing as roads cut a swath through the trees. Where once pilgrims walked through villages bringing with them useful income, now they ride quickly past in motor vehicles. Villagers used to make long journeys on foot, often carrying heavy loads on their backs. Roads have reduced this labor and increased their access to markets, schools, and hospitals, and to customers who buy their vegetables, fruit, baskets, and handicrafts. The downside is, as one village narrator commented, 'The people here are connected not with roads but with their forests. The grass will go, the trees will go, the stone will go from our village.'

While roads are changing the way of life in the forests, certain aspects of the culture endure. Forest villagers continue to observe their rituals of worship and festivals through fasting and prayers, music, singing, and dance. Special foods are served at these times, elaborate garlands and ropes of flowers are offered to the gods or worn over festive robes. Days are spent in careful preparation as homes are scrubbed until they shine; freshly washed courtyards are decorated with flower petals, colored powder or rice flour; scenes from the epics are painted on the walls and embellished with fragments of mirror; doorways are hung with mango leaves or marigold flowers. Each festival has its own particular foods and sweets according to the religion, season, and crops.

Above and opposite: Roads now cut through many of India's forests; this helps to link communities and makes getting carts to town or market easier. But these new thoroughfares can be a 'mixed blessing' for they also provide illegal loggers and poachers with better and faster access to their spoils.

RIVERS AND LAKES

India has so many rivers, lakes, and waterways. They are home to a wide variety of wild creatures and many are busy with boats and fishermen going about their trade. Tigers take a cooling swim, deer come to drink, birds strut and preen at the water's edge or wheel overhead. Sometimes, waterfalls tumble as rainbows dance in the spray. Temples are often erected on the banks. Except in the highest mountain peaks, farms, villages, and cities cluster next to the water for this is the hub of life and human activity.

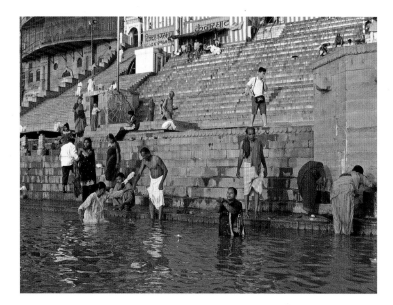

RIVERS AND LAKES

The subcontinent of India is criss-crossed by waterways many of which are home to much amazing wildlife. The name 'India' is, in fact, derived from the River Indus, where the earliest settlers made their homes in the surrounding valleys about 3000 years ago. Today the banks of India's rivers are the setting for many towns and villages; they bustle with both people and a wide variety of wildlife.

In this chapter we shall look first at India's most mighty rivers including the holy Ganges, the great loop of the Brahmaputra, and the historic Indus. Arising in the northern mountains and carrying rich alluvial soil to the plains below, for thousands of years these rivers have supported civilizations based on agriculture. Their snow-fed waters flow throughout the year but during the monsoon months of June to September, when heavy rain falls in the Himalayas and the rivers are very full, there are frequent floods in the low-lying plains.

Above: *Hindus, Buddhists, and Jains all consider the Ganges to be a holy river. Here, pilgrims descend the steep ghat steps to bathe in the Ganges at Varanasi in Uttar Pradesh.*

Right: *The reflection of the Jal Mahal (Water Palace) at Jaipur glows golden in a still lake that was once the site of royal duck-shooting parties.*

For such a vast land mass, India has very few natural lakes. In the Himalayas, lakes were created when glaciers either carved out a natural basin or deposited sufficient earth and rocks to create a natural dam across a river. Many of India's largest lakes are, in fact, reservoirs created in arid regions. In northwestern India, particularly in Rajasthan, there are several ephemeral salt lakes that are fed by intermittent streams and flash floods; once the rains vanish, the water evaporates to leave behind a layer of white salty soil. Udaipur in Rajasthan is often called the fairy-tale 'city of lakes' where calm lakes are ringed by wonderful opulent palaces that are reflected in the water.

Above: *Rajasthan and Punjab have many superb palaces and temples set beside beautiful, glittering lakes. The Golden Temple in Amritsar is one of the most splendid, surrounded by the peaceful 'Pool of Nectar.'*

Left: *Sandwiched between the Indus Valley and the main crest of the Indian Himalayas, the rugged scenery of this remote and inaccessible area is well guarded by snowy mountain passes and spectacular gorges. A popular trekking location, it is the setting for traditional villages and isolated Buddhist monasteries dating back to the 15th century.*

The Ganges

This is the most important river of the Indian subcontinent. Its river basin is India's largest measuring 400,000 sq miles (1 million km^2) in area and it is one of the world's most fertile and densely populated regions, covering some 25 percent of the nation's area – bounded by the Himalayas in the north and the older rounded mountains and hills of Vindhya to its south.

The Ganges (or Ganga) rises in the state of Uttaranchal where the Bhagirathi and Alaknanda headstreams have their source – the smaller Bhagirathi originates in the Gangotri Glacier at 25,446ft (7756m) high, and the Alaknanda near the Tibetan border below Nanda Devi's lofty peak at 25,646ft (7817m). Fed by melting snow and glacial ice, the two streams flow southward, converge and then travel 1560 miles (2510km) from the north-central Indian Himalayas through Bangladesh to the Bay of Bengal.

Above: *Rose and marigold petals on the Ganges – sometimes pilgrims make little 'boats' from dry leaves and place rice on them or, at night, float out tiny flickering oil lamps on the water.*

Right: *A boatman rows past the banks and steep ghat steps in Varanasi.*

First the Ganges flows past the city of Haridwar, famous for its temples and shrines. Then the river slides southeast across the Gangetic plain. Between Haridwar and Allahabad, it follows a winding course that is full of shoals and rapids. At Allahabad, the Yamuna river joins the Ganges and then this greater flow is further boosted by the Son river from the south and the Gumti, Ghaghra, Gandak, and Kosi rivers from the north. This ever-swelling river travels onward – through the cities of Mirzapur, Varanasi, Patna, and Bhagalpur, to skirt the Rajmahal Hills and then twist south to the head of the Ganges delta, some 560 miles (900km) downstream from Allahabad and about 280 miles (450km) short of the Bay of Bengal.

Near Pakaur the river divides: now the Bhagirathi separates to wind south and form the Hugli (Hooghly) river, a busy place where ocean-going vessels navigate the Bay of Bengal heading toward the port city of Kolkata (Calcutta). Meanwhile, the main branch of the Ganges continues through Bangladesh (for part of its course here becoming the Padma River). A vast network of waterways creates one of the globe's largest and most fertile deltas while the main river continues south – to be joined by the Brahmaputra and Meghna rivers (the name the confluence now assumes).

Finally, after passing some 52 cities and 48 towns, the now-massive river reaches the Bay of Bengal where the Meghna estuary measures 20 miles (30km) across. Its huge annual discharge of water is surpassed only by the Amazon and Congo rivers. Great deposits of sediment spread out from the delta into the bay. The Ganges basin is a vast, densely populated, and important agricultural region where rice, wheat and lentils, sugar cane, oil seeds, and potatoes are cultivated. An extensive canal system includes the Upper Ganges and Lower Ganges canals.

All along the banks of the Ganges – except where swampy mangrove forests spread their tangled roots into the water of the southwestern delta – are lakes and swamps where crops can be cultivated and jute, rice, sugar cane, legumes (fruits or seeds in pods), chilies, mustard, and sesame all thrive. The vast snow-capped peaks of the Himalayas provide the meltwater that keeps the Ganges flowing all year, and its abundant water is used for extensive irrigation too.

Left: Sunrise over the Ganges near the ancient holy city of Haridwar with its many temples – this is another place where pilgrims flock to take a ritual dip in the water to wash away sins.

Hindus consider the Ganges to be holy and it is named for Ganga, daughter of the mountain god Himavan or Himalaya. The river-water is used in many Hindu rituals and bathing in its sacred waters is said to wash away one's sins. In the hour before death, it is considered especially auspicious to drink from the Ganges. Many Hindus are cremated along its banks and their ashes are lowered into the river, especially at the holy city of Varanasi in Uttar Pradesh where some of the hundred or so ghats (flights of steps leading down to the river) serve as cremation sites. Most give access to the holy river for pilgrims wishing to bathe in the Ganges at this most sacred city – venerated by Buddhists and Jains as well as Hindus. Here are many temples including the Durga Temple, also known as the Monkey Temple. It is dedicated to the goddess Durga, the protector of the city, and is remarkable also for the number of monkeys that wander about its precincts.

Haridwar, where the Ganges leaves the Himalayas, is revered too and at sunset thousands of lamps are lit in the temples around the riverbank. Devotees float clay lamps on the river, asking the Mother Goddess for a wish. At Allahabad the mythical Saraswati river (which is mentioned in ancient Hindu texts) is said to enter the Ganges and the month-long Full Urn (*Purna Kumbh*) Festival is held in Haridwar and Allahabad every 12 years. Millions come to bathe in the Ganges then and to visit its holy sites and shrines, some near the river's headwaters. At Gangotri, under the glacier at an altitude of about 13,780ft (4200m) above sea level, one shrine marks the geographical origin of the Ganges. Here too is Gangotri Temple first built by the Nepalese soldier Amar Singh Thapa some 300 years ago.

The Ganga Puja festival celebrates Ganga Devi, the goddess of the River Ganges, and Jahnu Saptami the day when the sage Jahnu released the River Ganges after swallowing her. This is an especially propitious day to worship the Ganges and bathe in her waters and make offerings to the forefathers.

The Sundarbans offer a vast tract of forest and saltwater marshes in the lower part of the Ganges delta. Here the forest mutates into a mangrove swamp and the teeming estuaries are infested with crocodiles. This area is one of the last preserves of the Bengal tiger.

Above and top: Pilgrims and bathers throng at Varanasi, where many boats are moored. At least the Ganges is warmer here than at upriver holy sites where fast currents mean lifeguards must keep watch.

Opposite: The actual Ganges source is at Gaumukh but it is at Gangotri 12 miles (19km) away where pilgrims worship – for here legends claim the goddess Ganga descended to earth.

Brahmaputra river

This is one of the great rivers of southern Asia and its course runs at the highest altitude of any river in the world. It flows some 1800 miles (2900km) from its source on the slopes of Mount Kailash in southwestern Tibet's Himalayas to cross the Tibetan plateau, carving out a myriad channels and sandbanks on its way. Then, as it tumbles down from the Himalayan heights toward the plains of India, it twists back on itself, cutting a deep and unnavigated gorge, carving out many great ravines as it flows toward the Ganges. Now called the Dihang, the river turns south as it emerges in Arunachal Pradesh in northeast India, making a very rapid descent to lower altitudes and the plains where finally it becomes the Brahmaputra. It is joined by smaller rivers, and widens and flows all the way through Assam.

In between the Dibrugarh and Lakhimpur districts in Assam the river briefly becomes two channels surrounding one of the largest river islands in the world – Majuli. All along here are

Above: Padam men of the Adi tribe; 26 major tribes and many sub-tribes live in 3649 scattered villages in Arunachal Pradesh.

Top: The Brahmaputra river, known in Tibet as the Tsangpo, at first follows a slow gentle course en route to India.

tributaries and wetlands renowned for their rich flora and fauna including ducks and geese, pelicans, Siberian cranes, greater adjutant storks, and whistling teal. The river then narrows to cut through the rocks of the Shillong Plateau. The Brahmaputra splits into two branches in Bangladesh but these eventually re-converge and become part of the Ganges river system. It is the mingled waters of the two great rivers that flow out into the Bay of Bengal as the river Meghna. Many fishermen work along the banks of the river and near the delta mouth.

Navigable for most of its length, the Brahmaputra is one of the few rivers in the world to have a tidal bore. It is a popular place for shooting the rapids and river rafting trips can be experienced in the Arunachal Pradesh area. However, when the Himalayan snows melt in spring this river may flood – just like the Ganges – and create havoc for those who live and work on its banks. Each summer, swollen with monsoon rain, the Brahmaputra river inundates large parts of its surroundings, forcing people and animals to retreat to higher ground until the waters subside.

Above: Fishermen bring in nets as the sun sets near Guwahati in Assam. The city is situated in an area with many river islands and beaches.

Top: The Tsangpo, the world's highest major river, crosses the Tibetan plateau, carving out a myriad channels and skirting sandbanks.

Assam and its tribes

Much of the river's course runs through dense forests and past tribal settlements. People from many different races live along the banks of the Brahmaputra from Tibetans in the Himalayas to those with Mongol, Aryan, and Burman origins in Assam where Garo, Khasi, and Hajong tribes live in the hills. In the upper reaches, local people rear livestock while along the riverbanks rice is grown. Assam also has thriving tea, silk, and jute industries. Guwahati, its central hub and capital, is set in an amphitheater of forested hills and is an important river port and commercial center with an oil refinery and industries such as tea processing, agricultural products, and soap manufacture. It is also famous for its ancient Hindu temples.

The Bodo people were early settlers of Assam and are now members of a plains tribe that is one of the largest ethnic and linguistic groups of the Brahmaputra valley. They called the river Bhullam-buthur, which means 'making a gurgling sound,' a name that later mutated to its present and (unusually for a river) masculine name, taken from the Sanskrit words meaning 'son of Brahma.'

Large areas in Assam are covered with forests where the sal tree is a valuable source of timber and resin. The timber trade is important here. Tall reed jungles flourish in the swamps and low-lying marshy lands. Bamboos grow well and a variety of local handicrafts are made from this material. Many fruit trees blossom and bananas, papayas, mangoes, and jackfruit are cultivated.

Assam's enormous flood plain is a vital refuge for rare and endangered mammals including tigers, elephants, leopards, wild buffalo, jackals, sambar, hog and swamp deer, and the shy gaur, leopard cat, and sloth bear. The most important animal is the one-horned rhinoceros (*Rhinoceros unicornis*); the world's largest population of these animals live here (c.1850 individuals) and,

on the southern bank of the river, the Kaziranga Wildlife Reserve was established to protect it. It is now a national park encompassing large stretches of swamp, broad tracts of tall elephant grass, evergreen forests, watercourses and reedbeds, all teeming with wildlife including monitor lizards, rock pythons, and 483 species of bird.

Here wild boar crash through the undergrowth, otters fish in the pools, and the woodlands are home to many primates – capped-leaf monkeys (langur), macaques, and Hoolock gibbons as well as birds such as barbets, leafbirds, bulbuls, and warblers. Among the waterside's waving grasses are found herons, spot-billed pelicans, bar-headed geese, and storks (black-necked, adjutant, and lesser adjutant). Gray-headed or Pallas's fish-eagles and pied harriers hunt here, while gliding above Bengal floricans may be seen. These are small black and white bustards, and sadly its numbers are in serious decline, as are vultures that once flourished here; just four of the seven original species survive.

Above: A great one-horned rhinoceros in Kaziranga National Park, Assam; rhinos spend long hours in cool wallows or streams and may be seen on the Brahmaputra riverbanks.

Top: A large male elephant emerges from Assam's tall elephant grass that grows in dense clumps up to 10ft (3m) tall and often conceals the form of a mighty rhinoceros too.

Above left: Painted male dancers in Assam; many ritualistic folk dances developed from ancient cults and have magical significance.

Opposite: Mahatma Gandhi championed the teaching of basic literacy skills throughout India. Here primary schoolchildren in the Assam town of Makum learn to read and write in Hindu and Assamese – the easternmost Indo-European language that is spoken by over 13 million people.

Rivers and Lakes   115

The Indus river

India, the subcontinent's name, is derived from the Indus river that has its source in western Tibet with glacial streams from the Himalayas that join forces and flow northwest across parts of Jammu and Kashmir. This historic river ripples between the western edge of the Himalayan and Hindu Kush mountains, flowing north and west through Kashmir before it veers sharply to the south into Pakistan, cutting a gorge and pass that would become the ancient highroad into India – in due course invaded by armies from the west. The river drops south through Pakistan, eventually branching into a huge delta that covers some 3000 sq miles (7770km^2) and it enters the Arabian Sea southeast of Karachi. It has traveled a total distance of some 1800 miles (2900km) along the way, supplying essential water to irrigate millions of acres of arid land. It has 20 major tributaries including the Sutlej, Ravi, and Chenab.

The river has always been an important artery of traffic in a river valley that was the cradle of the ancient Indus civilization, which ranks with Mesopotamia and Egypt as one of the earliest civilizations, dating from around 3300 BC when it was one of the most significant areas of human habitation in the ancient world.

The river was crossed by Alexander the Great in 326 BC and then, at the end of the Indian campaign, Alexander's Greek army retreated along the southern course of the river back toward Persia. The Indus plains have, in their time, been dominated by the Persians, the Kushan empire, and Muslim armies and the river still acts as a natural boundary between the Indian hinterland and Afghanistan and Iran. Today there are many monasteries and temples raised on hills and ridges beside the riverbanks.

Long ago rich forest covered the length of Indus banks and the Mughal Emperor Babar writes of seeing rhinoceroses here. Sadly, intensive deforestation has left many regions as arid terrain with poor vegetation and people are dependent on irrigation schemes. However, the large delta creates a network of marshes, streams and creeks where marine fishes abound as the river meets the sea and there are still fishing centers beside the river.

India's major waterfalls

Chitrakot Waterfall, west of Jagdalpur in Chhattisgarh is sometimes referred to as India's answer to the Niagara Falls. This is the subcontinent's largest waterfall and it looks especially dramatic when the river Indravati abruptly collapses into a 100ft (30m) deep cavern. During and after the monsoon, when it is in full flood, the horseshoe-shaped waterfall is over 1000ft (nearly 305m) wide and flashes with dancing rainbows.

Farther east, the Barehipani Falls in Orissa is one of the tallest waterfalls in India. The water from the Budhabalanga river tumbles over a wide cliff, in two tiers, ending in a murky pool below and, in full flow, can create a violent tumult that in one place drops in a single tier a distance of 850ft (259m). It is part of a national park that is home to Bengal tigers.

The Jog Falls in Karnataka – in full flow from August to December – are the highest single-tier waterfalls in India (and second highest in Asia) at 830ft (253m). This water is divided into four distinct rushing cascades that drop directly down.

The water that reaches the falls at the spa town of Kutralam (or Courtallam) in the Western Ghats has passed through a forest full of herbs and so is believed to have medicinal properties. Its immense flow actually comprises nine waterfalls, and during the July monsoon an influx of visitors watch during the Saral festival as the water pummels the rocks and tiny droplets create a mist. Sometimes streaks of lightning flash across the sky above the festivities. Close by are the Five Falls, where the cascade spreads in five heads like a hooded cobra that resembles Adisesha, the serpent bearer of Lord Vishnu.

Above left: Waterfalls plummet at Jog Falls, Karnataka; its distinct rushing cascades are called Raja, Rani, Roarer, and Rocket.

Above right: The Kaveri river winds across the Deccan plateau, through rocks and ravines, then tumbles down the Shivanasamudra Falls.

Opposite: An aerial view of the tangle of channels at the Indus delta – 130 miles (210km) wide where it meets the ocean and occupying an area of some 16,000 sq miles (41,440km^2).

The Narmada river narrows between the silver and snow-white Marble Rocks (where the limestone is streaked with dark green or black volcanic veins) and then plunges down some 100ft (30m) as the breathtaking Dhuandhar Falls near Bhedaghat in Madhya Pradesh thunder over the rim.

Peninsular rivers

The subcontinent's main peninsular rivers (those that do not rise in the Himalayas) run farther south through the heart of India. The source of the Mahanadi lies at the southern edge of the Chhattisgarh plain but the headwaters of the other rivers catch the high rainfall of the Western Ghats and then traverse the plateau (mainly running from northwest to southeast) before reaching the Bay of Bengal. These peninsular rivers have relatively steep gradients and so, with the notable exception of the Krishna, are unlikely to rise above the margins of the river banks and flood their surroundings. Some, however, defy navigation with rushing rapids and dramatic gorges, especially as they cross the Eastern Ghats.

Peninsular rivers include the 910 mile (1465km) long Godavari that flows generally eastward from Trimbakeshwar in Maharashtra to the Bay of Bengal, passing through Andhra Pradesh. This river has been considered sacred for thousands of years. The revered scribe and sage Vyasa is believed to have composed the epic poem *Mahabharata* on the banks of the Godavari at the place now called Vyasara in his honor. Hindus visit several holy places along the river and may bathe in its sacred waters.

The Mahanadi (or Great River) runs its course from the Satpura mountains to the Bay of Bengal and flows through Chhattisgarh, Jharkhand, Orissa, and Maharashtra to attain an eventual length of 560 miles (900km). It has large dams that are used to generate hydroelectric power, and its mouth is the setting for the city of Puri, a famous pilgrimage site where the renowned Jagannath Temple is located.

The Kaveri (or Cauvery) is 475 miles (765km) long. It rises in the Western Ghats and meanders through the Coorg hills in Karnataka and Tamil Nadu on its way to the Bay of Bengal. This is another sacred Hindu river and encompasses the superb Shivanasamudra Falls, India's second biggest waterfall, as well as Abbey Falls in a lush green setting in the Western Ghats. The mouth of the river forms a large delta that is known as 'the garden of southern India.'

The Krishna rises near Mahabaleshwar in Maharashtra. It is considered an embodiment of the Hindu god Vishnu and its legendary source is a spout from the mouth of a cow statue in an ancient Mahadev temple there. It flows through Karnataka and Andhra Pradesh before finally draining into the Bay of Bengal about 800 miles (1300km) downstream. It is one of the longest rivers of India and its fast and furious flow can create soil erosion and disastrous floods during heavy monsoon rains. It is not navigable but provides water for irrigation schemes.

The Narmada forms a traditional boundary between north and south India and flows through India's only rift valley. It covers 800 miles (1300km) as its waters course from the Maikala range in Madhya Pradesh through Madhya Pradesh and Gujarat and then on to the Arabian Sea. It has always been an important route between the Arabian Sea and the Ganges river valley. So holy is this river that Hindus believe that just the sight of it will wash away all sins. At Hoshangabad its banks have beautiful ghats from which pilgrims bathe.

The Tapti rises in the Gawilgarh Hills of the central Deccan Plateau in south-central Madhya Pradesh, and ultimately drains into the Arabian Sea after running some 435 miles (700km) or so from east to west, passing the Melghat Tiger Reserve in Amravati and eventually reaching Gujarat. Legends claim that this river is the daughter of Lord Surya.

Below: A punt moves over flooded farmland. When torrential rains deluge India, dams may overflow and many rivers burst their banks to completely submerge their surroundings – flooding farms, villages, and towns.

Above: Pushkar lake is ringed by beautiful whitewashed temples and has long been a sanctified place of pilgrimage for Hindus. It is surrounded by 52 bathing ghats to which devotees flock in large numbers to take a dip in the lake.

Opposite: Pigeons flock around a white marble domed turret in Gaitor near Jaipur. This area is famous for the cenotaphs (chhatris) of Jaipur rulers, especially the glorious one for Maharaja Jai Singh II, made of white marble and decorated with carved peacocks.

Wetlands and lakes

India has a rich variety of wetland habitats including the pear-shaped Chilka Lake in Orissa. Asia's largest inland salt-water lagoon, this wetland is designated of international importance. It is separated from the Bay of Bengal by a sandy ridge and studded with small islands. Here, in a flourish of salmon pink, parades one of the world's largest breeding colonies of flamingos. It is also home to the Chilka dolphin. There are greylag geese, purple moorhens, jacanas, herons too – and white bellied sea eagles soaring above. Blackbuck, spotted deer, golden jackals, hyenas, and elephant herds inhabit the shores.

The lake is full of fish, prawns, and crab so fishing is an important industry here. Hundreds of small fishing craft set sail each morning with nets and bamboo traps from over 130 fishing villages that encircle the lake. When the lake shrinks in summer, women cultivate rice or millet here but, sadly, the recent use of motorboats and nylon nets is threatening the lake's resources.

Rajasthan's city of lakes

Rajasthan in the northwest has many majestic forts and opulent palaces. Here Udaipur (often referred to as the 'city of lakes' or the 'Venice of the East') was ruled by the Sisodia dynasty for 1200 years. Today it encapsulates a fascinating blend of fairy-tale palaces, temples, gardens, and narrow streets – all set beside glittering lakes.

The largest palace complex in Rajasthan is the granite and marble City Palace on Lake Pichola's eastern shore. It has a myriad fascinating architectural features – towers, cupolas, courtyards, pavilions, terraces, balconies, fountains, and gardens. The entry to the Palace is through three gates – the Elephant gate, the Big Gate, and then the Triple gate where the Maharaja would weigh out gold and silver to be distributed to the populace.

Close by is the gorgeous Jagdish Temple, consecrated to Lord Vishnu and built in 1651. On the shores of Lake Pichola there are bathing ghats where women still beat their washing with sticks, surrounded by hills, temples, and palaces, some built on islands so that they appear to float on the lake. To the north of Lake Pichola and linked by a gated canal, is Lake Fateh Sagar, a reservoir with hills on three sides, and containing three islands. Here are beautiful gardens, a boat-shaped café on Nehru Island, and a solar observatory on another isle. This lake is a major source of drinking water for the city of Udaipur.

The picturesque island palace of Jag Mandir is found on the southern island of Lake Pichola. It was built to provide a hideout for Prince Khurram (Shah Jahan) who was in conflict with his father. Here, as well as a row of superb elephant sculptures that look as though they are guarding the island, are beautiful cupolas and a domed pavilion. Its red sandstone was once studded with precious and semi-precious stones such as jasper, jade, and rubies. Inside are many elegant rooms, lavishly decorated with inlaid stones and rich paintings. Shah Jahan took refuge in this palace during 1623-24 and some sources claim that it inspired the design of the Taj Mahal, built in Agra from 1632 to 1648 as a mausoleum for the beloved second wife of Emperor Shah Jahan.

Above: All glistening white marble and mosaic,
Taj Lake Palace in Udaipur was built on an
island in 1746 for Maharana Jagat Singh II.

Opposite: Beautifully decorated elephants
often take part in ceremonial processions and
festivals in Rajasthan.

Top and center: *Bullocks, oxen, and elephants take part in Rajasthan festivals and may be spruced up in a lake first.*

Above and right: *52 sets of river landing stairs (ghats) lead down to the semicircular holy lake of Pushkar in Rajasthan.*

Salt lakes

India has several ephemeral salt lakes. Fed by short, intermittent streams, these become torrents during occasional intense rains when there may be flash floods. Afterward, once the rains have passed, the streams dry out. Then the water in the lakes evaporates too, leaving a layer of white saline deposits, from which a considerable amount of salt is extracted to be sold commercially.

Many of India's largest lakes are reservoirs that have been formed by damming rivers. West of Jaipur lies Sambhar, the subcontinent's largest salt lake – at full capacity 73sq miles (190km²) in area. Its inconsistent water depths fluctuate from about 1in (2.5cm) during the dry season to some 10ft (3m) or so after the monsoon. The algae and bacteria that thrive in these strange conditions sometimes turn the lake remarkable colors, while its edge is rimmed with a glittering frost of salt. This lake is also an important wetland at which thousands of migratory birds congregate.

Both the lake and nearby Naliasar Pond are key wintering areas for some 45 aquatic bird species including ducks, teals, bar-headed and graylag geese, storks, redshanks, sandpipers, coots, black-winged stilts, shovelers, pintails, large battalions of pelicans with their huge bills and thousands of flamingos. Sometimes up to 30,000 of these elegant birds feast on the algae that swarm in the lake when the saline conditions are just right.

Under a rocky outcrop jutting into the lake stands a small glimmering white temple that is dedicated to the goddess Shakambhari. According to legend she bestowed the lake upon the people of the area some 2500 years ago. Nearby, at Naliasar, terracotta figurines have been found and there is evidence of well-planned settlements dating back to the Kushan (1st – 3rd centuries AD) and Gupta (c. AD 320-600) periods.

Above: Pelicans catch fish by scooping them up in their vast expandable bill pouches, often while swimming on the surface of the water.

Opposite: A black-winged stilt in Keoladeo Ghana National Park where thousands of endangered birds gather each winter.

Ganesh festival

The God of good omens is Ganesh, the son of Shiva and Parvati who has an elephant's head and is worshiped by most Hindus as the god of wisdom and good fortune. His festival is celebrated widely in India, and particularly in the states of Maharashtra, Gujarat, Karnataka, and Andhra Pradesh when families and friends gather to eat *modak*, the famous sweet dumpling loved by the god, and to enjoy theater, art, and music performances. Clay models of Ganesh up to 26ft (8m) high are taken out in grand procession to the sound of cymbals and drums. The idols are finally immersed in a sea, lake, or river, notably in the Arabian Sea and Lake Powai (near Mumbai), Kankaria Lake near Ahmadabad, Sursagar Lake near Baroda, and the Sabarmati river. All these celebrations take place over ten or 11 days in late summer or early fall.

Above: An exuberant Hindu Festival at Mumbai honors Lord Ganesh, the elephant-headed god of wisdom and success. Huge images are taken out in grand processions and then immersed in the Arabian Sea. There are similar celebrations in many parts of India but they are especially splendid here.

Left and above left: Ganesh has an elephant's head and is usually depicted with a large round stomach, four arms, and a crown.

Opposite: Ganesh statues are taken through the streets in splendid style – accompanied by fanfares, dancing, and singing.

Waterside wildlife parks

Many of India's wildlife parks and sanctuaries encompass rivers and lakes, providing wonderful reserves for wildlife. For example, in Rajasthan's Ranthambore National Park (the former hunting ground of the Maharaja of Jaipur) some 50 or so aquatic plants flourish in lakes, streams, and watering holes – and here royal Bengal tigers come to drink. At the heart of the Periyar National Park and Tiger Reserve in Kerala is a lake and reservoir set between wooded hills. This perennial source of water attracts birds such as darters, cormorants, gray herons, ibis, and kingfishers plus sambar, gaur, and elephant herds. Even during the driest months of March and April, elephants can be seen bathing and swimming here.

Tigers come to drink too. Tigers and jaguars in South America, alone of all the big cats, love water and enjoy swimming but tigers do not like to get water in their eyes and often back into a water source to avoid this eventuality. They usually enjoy a good refreshing soak for about an hour and then settle on the bank to let the wind cool them further, before returning for another dip. Tigers are powerful swimmers and can cope with swiftly flowing currents. They can cross rivers up to 5 miles (8km) wide and have even been known to swim distances of up to 18 miles (29km).

Above: A royal Bengal tiger peeps out from the water as it enjoys a cooling bathe, oblivious to its endangered status.

Right: Ranthambore National Park is a good place to spot deer that often gather to graze in the shallow water at the edge of the lake.

Rhinoceros

The mighty Indian rhino (*Rhinoceros unicornis*) lives in many parts of the subcontinent, often favoring swampy riverside habitats where it feeds on plentiful water hyacinths. This is a free-floating plant, which grows up to 3.3ft (1m) in height and originates in the Amazon basin. It propagates very readily and creates great floating mats of vegetation that can become obstacles to navigation. The rhino eats grass and its well-developed upper lip helps it to crop the tall elephant grasses that it adores – as well as twigs, bamboo shoots, and reeds. It grazes mostly in the morning and evening and spends long periods during the hot day lying in water and wallowing in mud to cool off and to protect its hide from biting insects and sunburn.

This species, the most amphibious of the rhinos, is enormous at between 5.7 and 6.7ft (1.7 and 2m) tall and up to 13ft (3.9m) long. It is generally a peaceful animal, and is safe in its protective armor that consists of knobbly skin that falls into deep folds at its joints. The short blunt horn also serves to deter and threaten intruders. However, a rhino will charge to defend its territory and can run at up to 28mph (45kph) for short distances. Female rhinos sometimes whistle to attract a male's attention to form a bonding pair but generally these are mostly solitary animals.

The Indian rhino was once fairly widespread across much of the subcontinent but it is now endangered. Most are found in wildlife sanctuaries but poaching is still a threat as rhino horn is much sought after as an ingredient of medicine in the Far East where it sells for vast sums of money.

Once alarmingly reduced by hunting and poaching, rhino numbers have recovered since the Kaziranga National Park, which lies along the Brahmaputra river in Assam, became a wildlife conservation area in 1926 and, in 1940, was declared a sanctuary. Encompassing an area of about 166sq miles (430km²), its swamps and grasslands provide tall thickets of elephant grass and patches of evergreen forest to support the largest rhino population in the Indian subcontinent.

Above: *The rhinoceros lives in areas of tall grass, forests, and swamps – often wallowing in mud or marshy pools. It has excellent hearing and smell but rather poor eyesight.*

Playful otters

India is home to three species of otter: the Eurasian (*Lutra lutra*), the smooth-coated (*Lutra perspicillata*) and the small-clawed otter (*Amblonyx cinereus*). They live in rivers, lakes, ponds, streams, marshes, swamps, and rice paddy fields and may also be spotted in coastal inlets, mangrove swamps, estuaries and coves. Whatever their habitat, they do come up on land to nest. Otters are very playful. This helps young otters to develop co-ordination and also strengthens bonds within the group but they continue to play as adults – one of the few mammals to do so.

All have short, glossy, very dense fur. Unlike seals, otters do not have an insulating layer of body fat, so they rely on a soft, woolly undercoat covered by coarse guard hairs to keep them warm and dry. With five toes on each webbed paw, they paddle along but when swimming quickly or diving, they assume a streamlined shape by keeping the front paws close to their sides and using the longer back legs and powerful tail to propel them forward.

Otters relish fish, frogs, crayfish, crabs, and sometimes waterfowl, catching their prey with their mouths, not their forelimbs.

Occasionally they will make a meal of a rodent or rabbit. Indian smooth otters hunt as a family group, using teamwork to catch their prey. They may shelter for a while in shallow burrows, piles of rocks, or driftwood and some build permanent burrows near water, with an underwater entrance to a tunnel that leads to a chamber above the high-water mark. Sadly, pollution of waterways, draining of land for agriculture, and the trade in otter skins has greatly reduced their numbers.

Above: The Asian small-clawed otter is the world's smallest otter and it lives in rivers, creeks, and estuaries, patrolling territories marked with individual scent. It communicates with a repertoire of a dozen or so calls. Its rudimentary claws do not project beyond the forepaw toe pads and it uses these to feed on mollusks, crabs, and small aquatic creatures.

A world of water birds

Brahminy ducks or ruddy shelduck (*Tadorna ferruginea*) are considered sacred by Buddhists. With orange-brown body plumage and paler heads, they gather, especially at molting time, on slow streams and lakes and places like Sultanpur Bird Sanctuary in the Gurgaon district of Haryana, where demoiselle cranes, pelicans, flamingos, and shovelers also congregate.

The spot-billed pelican (*Pelecanus philippensis*) was a highly threatened species but is now happily on the increase in southern India where it nests in trees close to wetlands. These birds scoop up fish from the surface of the water into their large throat pouches that are covered in a spotted pattern, just like their bills, in the breeding season.

Keoladeo National Park near Bharatpur in Rajasthan has a rich network of shallow marshes, fed by the summer monsoon rains. The bird sanctuary here has wonderful boggy marshes as well as scrub and woodlands where pied kingfishers fly. It is home to both nesting indigenous and migratory water birds. Thousands flock here, including herons, painted storks, spoonbills, egrets, white ibis, and Siberian cranes and there are also large nesting colonies of the rare Indian skimmer.

Jacanas flaunt their iridescent colors, elegant tail feathers, and elongated legs and toes; they are sometimes called lily-trotters because they can nimbly trot across the tops of the floating aquatic plants on their extremely long toes. Here too are gorgeous mauve and turquoise feathered purple moorhens.

The gray, green, and red sarus crane (*Grus antigone antigone*) stands tall and elegant at around 5ft (155cm) in height – this is the world's tallest flying bird and the only resident breeding crane in India. About 8000 to 10,000 Indian sarus cranes survive today in India while Siberian cranes (*Grus leucogeranus*) are rare visitors and the pride of this sanctuary. Only some 125 pairs of these pure white, crimson-billed cranes are believed to survive worldwide. If alarmed, the cranes spring into flight, sometimes reaching speeds of 52mph (84kph) but usually they soar in the thermal updrafts to some 5000ft (1500m) or so – and far higher when migrating over mountains.

Cranes forage for roots and tubers as well as eating seeds, small mammals, reptiles, eggs, worms, clams, insects, and crayfish. They may sprint to chase small prey, taking up to three steps every second and using their wings for balance; they can easily outrun a human. In between these bursts of activity, they spend a good deal of time preening, nibbling the base of a feather and then drawing it through the bill – every now and then applying oil to their plumage from a gland at the top of the tail.

Above: The painted stork catches fish (and sometimes frogs and snails too) by swinging its partly open bill through the water, until something suitably tasty drifts inside.

Left: Pelicans fly across a lake as the sunset's glow fades from the sky.

Opposite: Normally ruddy shelduck live in pairs or small groups but, in winter, larger flocks gather on lakes or slow-moving rivers.

The Indian cormorant or Indian shag (*Phalacrocorax fuscicollis*) gathers in colonies at the edge of rivers, lakes, and wetlands throughout the subcontinent, except around the highest Himalayan peaks. In the breeding season the adults are glistening black with white speckles on the head and neck and white feathery tufts behind the eyes. They usually feed in shallow water, but they can dive deep, and cormorants secured by leashes have been used to fish on behalf of their human captors in some Indian communities in the past – a practice that survives today in China and Japan.

Up above the marshes, hungry harriers and fishing eagles keep a sharp lookout for tasty morsels including many types of turtle. The marshes also offer a home to the highly endangered Gangetic river dolphin, marsh crocodiles (muggers), and gharials – that can be seen both here and at the Chambal Bird Sanctuary – where sambar, nilgai, wolves, and wild boar also roam, sharing this bountiful habitat with some 260 bird species.

Above: Little, great, and cattle egrets join hundreds of birds on the marshes and lakes of Sultanpur National Park, near Delhi.

Above and right: Demoiselle cranes must cross the mighty Himalayas to reach their winter refuges in northwest and central India: eastern Rajasthan, Gujarat and Madhya Pradesh. They fly in disciplined order with heads, necks, feet, and legs held straight, announcing their arrival with noisy 'krok-krok' calls as they descend to marshes or river sandbanks.

Taj Mahal

Within 43 miles (70 km) of Chambal Bird Sanctuary is the city of Agra and the world-famous Taj Mahal. Built on the banks of the river Yamuna, it is believed that the river itself was incorporated into the design of the gardens and was meant to be seen as one of the rivers of Paradise. Linked to the Ganges, the river provides a dramatic backdrop to this majestic building where the calm water provides a mirror and the shimmering reflections create a mirage of a floating tomb, which is further accentuated by the water channels in the gardens.

The mausoleum is made of white marble and seems to alter in color as changing seasons and times of day are reflected in its brilliant surfaces. It has a pink glow in the morning, is milky white as evening descends and golden in moonlight when semi-precious stones inlaid into the marble twinkle like stars – changes that may depict a woman's different moods. It was built in memory of Shah Jahan's beloved wife Mumtaz Mahal who died in childbirth in 1631.

Elephant power contributed to the raising of this great edifice. A fleet of more than 1000 elephants helped to transport construction material from all over India and central Asia to the site – a task that took 22 years, from 1631 to 1653. The river also played an important role in its construction, transporting building materials and providing sand and shingle from the river bed to be used in the building works.

Above and right: A long reflective pool and minarets add grandeur and mystery to the main facade of the Taj Mahal. It can also be seen from the Yamuna river. This beautiful building embodies the romantic spirit of India.

Right: India's rivers are greatly revered, a symbol of her long culture and civilization – ever changeable, sometimes unpredictable and dangerous, but more often life-giving and generous, the source of fertility for the land and enrichment of the human spirit.

Below: Many throng to the Varanasi ghats early, there to offer their morning prayers to the rising sun.

In conclusion

India's rivers, both great and small, her lakes – freshwater and saltwater, natural and artificial – her many pools, swamps, and wetlands… all throng with a multitude of creatures that make their homes here, while birds and waders mass at the fringes or fly overhead. In a country that offers so much diversity of landscape and wildlife, it is the silver threads of waterways and the deep blue and turquoise of its still lakes that carry the precious gift of water to the natural world, the liquid upon which all life depends. This is a vital commodity for, despite the deluges of the monsoon season, the summers are hot and the land relies on these fluid-filled veins and arteries to keep its pulse alive and beating strongly.

PLAINS AND DESERTS

South of the Himalayas, India reveals vast swaths of desert and green plain and many an exotic
glittering city. In the arid northwest, the Great Indian Desert shimmers under the hot sun or dances in
a dust storm while sand dunes, palaces, forts, and camels give Rajasthan its special romantic flavor.
In other regions barren salt flats are visited by noisy migratory birds, while sweeping plains stretch
from riverside to hill – cultivated for thousands of years with crops like rice, sugar cane, tea, and cotton.
A myriad golden and emerald landscapes await . . .

PLAINS AND DESERTS

Beyond the banks of India's rivers, flatter areas stretch between the watercourses and the higher ground of hills or mountains. Set in the country's heartland, India's plains are mainly fertile cultivated areas, often with underground water reserves. With a total landmass of 1,147,955sq miles (2,973,190km²), the vast plains of the subcontinent include the Indo-Gangetic Plain, the Central Highlands, the Great Indian Desert, and the Rann of Kutch.

The state of Madhya Pradesh straddles the Narmada river and is home to a large tribal population. Its rugged north is famous for its Khajuraho temples, magnificent edifices constructed between AD 950 and 1050 during the Chandel Empire and decorated with wonderful sculpture – some of it very erotic. Set farther west in the great plains lies Gujarat where many Jain temples are found. This was the chief center of wood carving in India from at least the 1400s. It is set in plains that stretch over some 12,800sq miles (33,000 km²), bounded by the Arabian Sea to the south and the desert fringe of Rajasthan to the northeast.

Above: Vishwanath temple, Khajuraho, enshrines a three-headed image of Lord Brahma; lions and elephant sculptures flank the entrances. Some 85 medieval temples were built here from 950 to 1050 but only 22 survive.

Right: Rajasthan nomads keep sheep, goats, and cattle while some breed camels. Many people here are great storytellers or musicians.

The vast plains of Kutch also extend to Rajasthan, which is renowned for its colorful desert festivals and palaces. India's plains can be incredibly hot with searing summer temperatures that may soar above 108°F (42°C), but it is not all desert in Rajasthan. In its southwestern reaches, the land is green and fertile; millet, wheat, maize, and cotton are grown and there are rich wetlands in Keoladeo Ghana National Park.

The Malabar coastal plains in the south are well-cultivated – crops such as coconut, betel, pepper, coffee, and tea all grow here. The Punjab plains in the northwest are also cultivated to grow cereals, oilseeds, cotton, and sugar cane, while the plains of Kutch, farther south, are sandy with rocky hills and cliffs. Kutch has long been a significant meeting point for different races and people including many nomadic pastoralists, Hindu cattle-breeders, and shepherds. The Great Rann of Kutch (a marshy region during the monsoon that lies next to the border with Pakistan) dries out in summer to a barren plain. A major earthquake in 1819 altered the course of the Indus river and created a surface depression here that ultimately became an inland sea.

Above: Herdsmen move their stock across a dry stony plain where water is precious. Extensive irrigation projects include canals, village ponds, wells, and tanks.

Left: There is no shortage of rain here. Heavy summer downpours swamp the land and turn parts into shallow lakes. The women have rolled up their saris as they work in the waterlogged rice fields.

The Indo-Gangetic Plain

The large and fertile Indo-Gangetic Plain encompasses a large chunk of northern and eastern India, an area of some 270,000sq miles (700,000km²) – bound to the north by the mighty Himalayas: their glaciers, snows, and streams feed its numerous rivers and deposit rich fertile soil and sediments. Long, long ago this was a seabed, but this plain is now filled with vast quantities of alluvium (or river-borne sediment) – the most extensive tract of uninterrupted alluvium on the globe.

The plain stretches from Pakistan in the west (where it is watered by the Indus and its tributaries) ever eastward to the Brahmaputra valley in Assam and the Bay of Bengal in the east. At its southern edge lies the Deccan plateau and on the India–Pakistan border – and considered a part of the plain – is the arid Thar Desert.

Not only are the Ganges plains highly fertile but they also contain some of the largest reserves of underground water in the world – perfect for well irrigation and canals. Such natural riches have encouraged farming, settlement, and, ultimately, the construction of towns and cities too. The Indo-Gangetic Plain is highly populated: some 900 million people (over 13 percent of the world's population) live here in one of the most densely populated areas in the world.

Above: *A typical town; Neolithic cultures arrived in the south c.8000 BC.*

Right: *Rice grows well in the fertile lowlands; summer rainfall turns the Indo-Gangetic plain into a 'grain bowl,' producing 50 percent of the nation's rice and wheat.*

Delhi: history, food, and festivals

The origins of the city of Delhi may well be traced back more than 5000 years. People have been living in the area since at least 2000 BC and probably even earlier than that. This is one of the most ancient cities that still survives and thrives – but not in its original form for it has been built and destroyed many times over and the remains of at least seven major cities have been discovered here. It is referred to in the Indian mythological epic *Mahabharata* as Indraprastha (meaning the City of Indra), but historic records begin rather later.

The Tomar Rajputs were credited with founding Delhi proper in AD 736; it was the capital of several ancient empires and a vital element in the trade routes that stretched from northwest India across the Gangetic plains. Old Delhi (or the Old City) was rebuilt by the Mughals; from the 1500s, their empire dominated

Above: *The Indian Army Camel Corps on parade on Republic Day in Delhi. Horses and elephants also march, medals are awarded to the military and the Indian Air Force stages spectacular fly-pasts.*

northern India for over three centuries. Later the British architect Edwin Lutyens constructed a new metropolitan district called New Delhi and this became the administrative headquarters for the British Raj. In 1947, New Delhi was declared the capital of India when the nation became independent of British rule.

Countless ancient monuments and archaeological sites remain, such as the 1648 Red Fort – the Mughal emperor Shah Jahan's palace – a glowing pink sandstone fortress with its imposing Lahore Gate. Once its walls were inlaid with gems while its pavilion boasted a silver ceiling encrusted with precious gems. The Rang Mahal housed royal wives and concubines; it has a lotus-shaped fountain made from just one piece of marble. Emperor Shah Jahan was responsible for another fine edifice, India's largest mosque, the sandstone and marble Jama Masjid, completed here in 1656. It cost a million rupees and was the work of 5000 artisans.

Above: At one end of Rajpath stands India Gate, a majestic arch, 138ft (42m) high. It houses an eternal flame that burns to commemorate the Unknown Soldier and countless warriors who have lost their lives in World War I and the Afghan war. It looks especially striking when illuminated at night.

Opposite above: The Red Fort was a fortress palace built 1639–48 in Delhi, which was then called Shahjahanabad. It was named for the Mughal emperor Shah Jahan when he moved his capital here from Agra. There are domed and arched marble palaces, plush private apartments, a mosque, beautiful paintings, gold, silver, and mosaics everywhere – and wonderful gardens.

Delhi boasts the world's tallest sandstone minaret, the Qutub Minar; 238ft (72.5m) high, its construction dates from the time of the first Muslim kingdom in India. It was begun in 1193 and the last story was completed in 1368. The National Rail Museum explores the history of India's incredible railways that cover 39,370 miles (63,360km) while the dramatic India Gate at the center of New Delhi is India's answer to the Arc-de-Triomphe in Paris. It stands at great highway crossroads as a memorial to fallen soldiers, in this case 90,000 lost when fighting for the British Army during World War I and in the 1919 Afghan war. However, Delhi is not just about history: skyscrapers coexist comfortably with the ancient forts and tombs and there are modern shopping malls as well as colorful bazaars.

Delhi is a hub of India's traditional festivals including January's celebration of kite-flying on the green lawns at Connaught Place while January 26 marks the inauguration of the Republic of India in 1950. Here in Delhi the celebrations include a magnificent parade of the Armed Forces, folk dances, and decorated floats from the different states. Holi, the festival of colors, is celebrated in March as people smear gulal (colored powder) on their faces and dance as drums beat out a compulsive rhythm.

The three-day celebration of Id-Ul-Fitr signifies the end of Ramadan, a period of worship, contemplation, and fasting that occurs during the ninth month in the Islamic calendar year. Id-Ul-Fitr is a festival of spiritual love and sharing when the fast is broken and special foods and delicacies are prepared to be distributed to friends and neighbors.

Independence Day is celebrated on August 15 when there are processions and a flag is hoisted on the Red Fort. Dussehra, a ten-day festival, takes place in September or October when the heroic deeds of Lord Rama are enacted in song and dance and huge effigies of Ravana, the demon king, are burnt on the final day.

The Diwali festival of lights and fireworks is celebrated throughout the nation usually at the end of October or the beginning of November. Houses are illuminated with rows of earthen lamps to welcome Lakshmi, the goddess of wealth and prosperity. At night there are fireworks to celebrate the return of Lord Rama from exile. Makar Sankranti is a mid-winter festival with bull fights and bullock races and is the time when millions of pilgrims in the eastern region immerse themselves for religious reasons in the Ganges.

Above: A busy bazaar spills along the old Delhi streets – already lined with shop goods cascading out onto the pavements in a colorful hotchpotch of fabric, jewelry, carpets, spices, and enticing foods.

Opposite above: Ornate arches and pillars enrich the splendid interior of the Red Fort where there is opulent use of marble, mosaic, and decorative features. Many rooms served specific purposes including one 'chamber for counting beads for private prayer.' Originally six marble palaces graced the eastern waterfront.

Opposite below: Set beside carved columns taken from ancient Hindu temples, the red sandstone tower Qutub Minar (meaning pole or axis), is the world's tallest brick minaret. It stands on the site of North India's first Muslim kingdom – established in 1193 – and is covered with intricate carvings and verses from the Koran.

Above and top: Street vendors sell peanuts (roasted as you watch) – as well as bananas, hot chapatis, vegetable curries, jalebi (deep-fried batter in syrup), pani puri (hollow dough stuffed with spicy potatoes and chutney), steaming hot samosas, and kulfi (frozen milk flavored with almonds and saffron amongst other ingredients).

Delhi is a good place to sample northern India's cuisine, in particular tandoori dishes baked in clay ovens, and biryani – rice with chicken or meat cooked in a clay pot – plus countless mouthwatering chutneys and pickles, roti, naan and mint breads, lentil specialties, kofta meatballs and traditional delicacies often served in small bowls on a platter (a *thali*). Meat, fish, and vegetables may be given extra flavor by marinating them in yoghurt and spices. Desserts include a scrumptious saffron and pistachio ice cream.

Above: Cooking on the streets in Delhi is soon to be banned, which will threaten many traditional family businesses.

Top: Food is served in rooftop cafes, at busy street stands, palatial restaurants or, as here, in the omnipresent dhaba.

Left: A Bangalore market offers a profusion of choice. India is a major fruit and vegetable producer and exporter.

These pages: Holi, the Hindu festival of colors, is celebrated with great exuberance. Everyone chases around, throwing brightly colored powder (gulal) and water over each other and then singing and dancing in the streets. In Jaipur the famous elephant festival precedes Holi.

Amritsar and Lucknow

Another amazing metropolis is Amritsar, a holy city in the Punjab lying close to the Pakistan border. It is named after the holy pool of the nectar of immortality around the Golden Temple (the Harmandir Sahib) complex, and is the spiritual and cultural center of the Sikh religion. Set among a maze of lanes and 18 fortified gateways, this is a city within a city – begun by Guru Ram Das, the fourth Sikh Guru, and completed in 1601 by his successor, Guru Arjan Dev. It is resplendent with gold leaf and white marble, with a gold-covered dome and a hall of mirrors where the floors are swept by a brush made from the finest peacock feathers.

During the late 1700s Lucknow (in the state of Uttar Pradesh) was a great cultural center, where music and dance flourished under the patronage of the wealthy nawabs. Here many wonderful architectural gems include the magnificent Qaiser Bagh Palace, the Royal pleasure gardens of Sikander Bagh, the haunting ruins of the British Residency where British people sought refuge during the Indian Mutiny of 1857, and the elegant Bara Immambara complex – a Muslim ceremonial hall with elaborate gates, balconies, a labyrinth of passages, and a mosque.

Above: Guards stand before the Golden Temple (Harmandir Sahib) in Amritsar. This is the holiest Sikh shrine, built 1589–1604. Here the Holy Book is kept under a jeweled canopy.

Left: The Golden Temple has a gold, inverted-lotus-shaped dome. There is marble, silver, gold-leaf animal and flower decoration – and the entire temple is surrounded by a large lake of water.

Tripura Plains

The Tripura Plains of northeastern India cover some 1600sq miles (4150km²), a landlocked hilly area almost surrounded by Bangladesh, and dotted with lakes, marshes, and forests that provide timber, bamboo, firewood, charcoal, and rubber. Tripura, possibly named after a legendary tyrant king, was an independent Hindu kingdom for more than 1300 years before it acceded to India in 1949. Most people in this mainly rural community are Hindus, with some inclusion of Muslims, Buddhists, and Christians.

Rice is the major crop but jute, cotton, tea, pineapples, jackfruits, and oranges are also carefully nurtured, as well as livestock such as cattle, buffalo, sheep, goats, pigs, and poultry. There are many cottage industries too – weaving, carpentry, basketry, and pottery – with the production of tea, sugar, sawn timber, bricks, glass, and furniture assisting the local economy.

Nearly 400 species of trees grow here. The Sepahijala Wildlife Sanctuary is home to about 150 species of birds as well as the rare Phayre's langur (*Trachypithecus phayrei*) or leaf monkey, often called the bespectacled monkey because it has white rings of fur arching around its eyes. It stays high up in the foliage, collecting dew or water from rain-drenched leaves so that it need never leave the safety of the treetops where it jumps from branch to branch looking for leaves, buds, and fruits on which to feed.

Trishna Wildlife Sanctuary is renowned for its gaur (bison) as well as deer, Hoolock gibbons and many langurs – golden, capped, and spectacled. The area fairly bustles with reptiles too as well as rhesus monkeys, wild boar, leopards, and other wild cats. Birds here include pheasant-tailed jacanas, red jungle fowl, white breasted kingfishers, the superb glossy Indian black drongo, jungle mynas, eagles, hornbills, and the tailorbird, that pierces and sews a large leaf with plant fiber or a thread of a spider's web to form a cradle support for its grass nest.

Above: Harvesting rice – this is one of the most important staple crops, providing food for billions of people worldwide. India produces some 112 million tons. Rice is not really an aquatic plant but grows well in flooded fields where submersion in water helps to control otherwise invasive weeds.

Opposite above: Zebu in the Thar Desert – an ancient cattle breed, humped zebu were being domesticated in western Asia by 6000 BC and they then spread across the continent.

Opposite below: The white-throated kingfisher has a blue back, wings, and tail but the head, shoulders, and front are a gorgeous chestnut, except for the white breast. It hunts large insects, rodents, snakes, frogs, and fish.

Life on the plains

Asian elephants were once widely dispersed across the subcontinent but now they number only about 45,000 individuals. Much of the fertile alluvial plains have been cleared and intensely cultivated, so now there is little natural forest left and the fauna and flora are inevitably greatly diminished. Once there were many tigers, greater one-horned rhinoceroses, Asian elephants, wild water buffalo, swamp deer, sloth bears, and hornbill species – but these creatures need abundant space and have been largely driven away by the relentless destruction of their habitat. Those that survive in scattered protected areas include tigers, Asian elephants, wild boar, and sloth bears.

Here too in the wetlands and forest habitats are found several species of deer. The chousingha (*Tetracerus quadricornis*) is a type of shy antelope that stands only 1.8-2.1ft (55-65cm) tall. They live generally solitary lives in the forest and are rarely found far from water. The males grow four horns which are never shed but during the rutting season when the males compete to mate with the females, the horns may be damaged and break off. A type of swamp deer, the barasingha (*Cervus duvaucelii*), of which only some 4000 survive in the world, are now only found in isolated protected forests and marshes in Uttar Pradesh, Assam, and Madhya Pradesh. Their pale-yellow to dark-brown coats afford them good camouflage among the tall elephant grasses but poaching for their large antlers, and the loss of vital forest habitats, means that they are now endangered. They keep their precious fawns well hidden in the world's tallest grasses.

Although only some 35in (90cm) tall, the wild boar (*Sus scrofa cristatus*) is renowned for its incredible sense of smell, determination, and courage; it is one of the few creatures with

the nerve to challenge a tiger. It sports a pair of long sturdy canines that grow upward and outward and a ridge of thick bristle-like hairs running from the nape of its neck to its posterior. Once there were some six or seven species found in the subcontinent, but today only a single species survives. Meanwhile, the hundred or so tuskless pygmy hogs (*Sus salvanius*), found only in Assam, are the world's smallest pigs, weighing about 9lb (8.5kg).

Birds include the Bengal florican (*Houbaropsis bengalensis*). The male performs a rather comical breeding dance, jumping from a

single spot in the tall grasses into the air in repeated vertical take-offs. Although only some 18in (45cm) tall, it jumps about 4ft (1.2m) into the air, rattling or clapping its wings, and then floating down again with its tail spread out. It performs this ritual up to 500 times a day to advertise its presence to potential mates and to warn off any rivals.

Oriental pied hornbills (*Anthracoceros albirostris*) live in forested regions here too as do Indian gray hornbills (*Ocyceros birostris*) that nest in tree holes. The female hornbill, sealed inside to safeguard both eggs and chicks, plucks out all her feathers and

Above: The total number of wild Asian water buffalo may be less than 4000; they are classified as critically endangered. The domestic Asian water buffalo is, however, plentiful and is used to pull carts and as a dairy animal.

Opposite: The female nilgai has a short yellow-brown coat. The adult horned male has a bluish slate-gray coat, looks slightly like an ox and is sometimes known as a blue bull. In fact, this is Asia's biggest antelope.

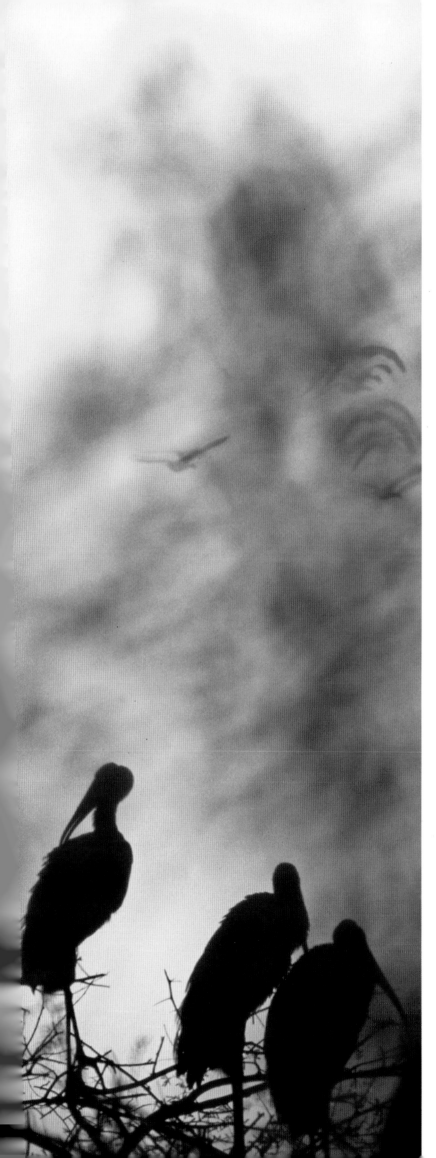

deposits these outside to conserve space within the nest for her growing brood. Her feathers re-grow to coincide with the chicks leaving the confines of the brood 'prison.'

There are also storks (painted, white-necked, and black), peafowls, crested serpent eagles, Bonelli's eagles, Indian horned owls, quails, partridges, jacanas, and Asian paradise flycatchers with black crested heads, gorgeous chestnut feathers and very long flamboyant tail streamers. India's beautiful blue-tailed and green bee-eaters sometimes steal grapes and figs as well as catching bees on the wing. Indian rollers may be seen performing a spectacular tumbling flight, rolling over and over. At other times they spread their brilliant blue and turquoise wings and simply soar.

Some people claim that the monitor lizard, found throughout India, is so intelligent that captive specimens have been taught to count, and there are tales of wild lizards warning people of the presence of crocodiles in the vicinity. An agile climber and swimmer, it has a long heritage (it is related to the mosasaur, a 33ft/10m-long marine lizard that lived over 65 million years ago). It threatens enemies by gaping, inflating its neck and hissing, while spreading its ribs to expand its body. It can dismember and gulp down prey and may rise up on its hind legs before attacking, sometimes by delivering a well-aimed blow with its powerful tail.

Above: Once in soaring outstretched flight, the painted stork is safe from terrestrial predators like tigers, leopards, hyenas, and crocodiles.

Left: Nesting storks lay their eggs on a platform of sticks in trees or mangroves and then stand guard over the offspring.

Deccan plateau

South of the Indo-Gangetic Plain, the Deccan plateau and peninsula is geologically the oldest landmass in India. It is set mainly some 1000 to 2500ft (300 to 760m) above sea level and is separated from the Gangetic plain by mountain ranges. Flanked by the Eastern and Western Ghats, this huge elevated tableland occupies a large part of southern India and extends over eight states.

Here splendid waterfalls and cascades include the Hogenakkal Falls and the Sivasamudram Falls where the river Cauvery cascades down from a height of 320ft (98m) and rushing white waters plunge into a deep rocky gorge. Nearby, a group of ancient temples add to the atmosphere.

Meanwhile, set in lush tropical jungle in Goa are the Dudhsagar Falls, India's fifth tallest at 1017ft (310m) – tumbling over the Deccan plateau in spectacular fashion during the monsoons.

The Deccan is home to people of many cultures and languages who live in hills along the northern and northeastern edges of the plateau. Cotton, sugar cane, and rice are grown but the plateau has other even more lucrative riches to offer: mica and iron ore – plus gold and diamonds in the Golconda region near Hyderabad. The largest city here is Bangalore, once a center of colonial rule, now a manufacturing hub and the home of India's 'silicon valley' where ancient buildings like the ornate Bull Temple contrast with the gleaming glass corporate offices and headquarters that serve new technologies.

This ecoregion is home to several threatened mammals including some 600 elephants that range from the Nilgiri Hills to the Eastern Ghats – this is the largest single elephant population in India; another group roams the Anaimalai and Nelliampathi Hills. Here too are tigers, wild buffalo, wild dogs, sloth bears, chousingha, gaur, chinkaras, blackbucks, and Malabar squirrels.

The grizzled giant squirrel (*Ratufa macroura*) is classified as an endangered species. It builds a pair of 'safety nets' in the forks of branches of adjacent tree crowns so that it can confuse predators like birds and snakes by leaping from one tree to another if threatened. It uses one net as a nursery and the other for just resting in after spending the day eating fruit, nuts, insects, birds eggs, and the bark of some trees.

Sadly, continual habitat loss and hunting means that populations of all these creatures are diminishing, including the endangered Salim Ali's fruit bat which is one of the rarest bats in the world. First collected in 1948 it was misidentified and only recognized as a new species in 1972 when it was named after Salim Ali, a well-known Indian ornithologist. There are also almost 300 bird species in the region, including the globally threatened Jerdon's courser (*Rhinoptilus bitorquatus*), which was rediscovered in 1986 after 80 years when there were no sightings. It is so rare and shy that virtually nothing is known of its habits.

Opposite: The Sivasamudram (or Cauvery) Falls encompass both a large horsetail waterfall and a cascade, which tumble down into dense swirling clouds of mist.

Left: India's blackbuck antelopes are fast sprinters on the open plains and can outrun most predators. The males have superb, spiraling ridged horns.

Forts and sanctuaries

Surrounded by the Vindhya and Aravali hill ranges and close to the outer fringes of the Thar Desert, Ranthambore National Park is borderland terrain, with an area of deciduous forest, as well as plains near the hills – and desert areas too. The Maharaja of Jaipur once hunted in the deciduous forest of this park, now especially renowned for its royal Bengal tigers but a good number of leopards roam here too, as well as jackals, mongooses, sloth bears, wild boar, porcupines, foxes, caracals (lynx-type cats), hyenas, gazelles, Indian hares, marsh crocodiles, and lizards.

Ranthambore fort is located in a strategic position on top of a rocky outcrop, commanding spectacular views of what is now Ranthambore National Park. It was built by the Chauhan rulers in the 900s and is one of the oldest forts of Rajasthan. Due to its position and construction, this huge fort was considered to be one of the most difficult to overthrow. It was a fiercely contested seat of power for many rulers and the site of some of the bloodiest battles in Indian history. Legends tell how in 1303 the royal women here committed suicide rather than face capture and disgrace when Muslim invaders led by Ala-ud-din Khilji laid siege to the fort.

At Rajasthan's Gajner Wildlife Sanctuary, the lake and forested hills are inhabited by wildfowl, hares, wild boar, desert foxes, deer, blackbucks, and blue bulls or nilgai (*Boselaphus tragocamelus*). In fact these are not bulls at all but antelopes. In winter, thousands of water birds, including flocks of Imperial sand geese, swoop down to a lake below the former hunting lodge of the great Maharaja Ganga Singh of Bikaner.

Above: Sambar deer wade below the vast 1000-year-old Ranthambore fort. Once, more than a thousand women committed mass suicide here after a battle and, in the 1600s, executions involved throwing opium-dazed prisoners over the rocky outcrop.

Opposite: Temple pillars, Ranthambore – there are many splendid ruins in Ranthambore park, once a maharaja's hunting ground.

Camels and festivals

Many Hindus, Muslims, and Sikhs live in the Thar (or Great Indian) Desert and the people here maintain a colorful culture, rich in tradition, music, and poetry. An annual desert festival is celebrated in February in Jaisalmer in the state of Rajasthan. The local people, wearing brilliant costumes, perform folk dances and sing haunting ballads, while snake charmers, puppeteers, acrobats, and camel races add to the fun. There are competitions for the best-dressed camel, as well as for the man with the finest mustache and for turban tying.

Bikaner, Pushkar, and Jaisalmer fairs are all spectacular occasions involving bedecked (and sometimes dancing) camels, decorated cattle, competitions, fire dancers who balance burning lamps on their foreheads, processions, skirt-swirling dancers, and dazzling fireworks. Pushkar is also a major site for Hindu pilgrims who bathe in Pushkar lake while the busy winding streets throng with people stopping by market stalls selling camel saddles, textiles,

silver, and jewelry. Beyond, on the fringe of the vast desert, thousands of camels wait as families set up camp. There are craft bazaars, a sound-and-light spectacle and a glittering grand finale that takes place in the silvery moonlit sand dunes on the night of the full moon.

Nearby is a camel research farm and breeding center for several thousand camels – a unique project in Asia – set in over 3sq miles (8km^2) of semi-arid terrain. Turbaned Rabari herdsmen tend the camels and eventually many of the camel offspring, decorated in their finest camel trappings, are sold at the fairs.

Above: Camels and their owners gather at Pushkar in Rajasthan during the desert festivals, ready for celebrations, music, and races.

Opposite: Festivities take place in the Sam Desert near Jaisalmer, which is famous for its sand dunes, camel safaris, and moonlit events.

Above, right, and opposite: Rajasthan is the scene of many colorful ceremonies that take place every January or February when the winter festivals are celebrated with great enthusiasm by huge numbers of people, with lots of music, dance, and acrobatics. Camels feature strongly – in special camel races, camel polo, and camel dances. All the local people wear brilliant costumes – and enjoy the fun that continues late into the night. The desert is busy with brightly painted stalls, tents, carpet sellers, and crafts bazaars. There are performances by snake charmers, puppet shows, folks songs, ballad renderings. Competitions include those for the finest mustache and turban tying – both important badges of honor here – as well as one for the camel judged to be sporting the finest apparel.

Following pages: Enthusiastic dancing in colorful costumes swirling out in flashes of bright yellow, red, pink, and green.

The Rann of Kutch

Kutch (meaning turtle) is a dome-shaped landmass in Gujarat, cut off from mainland India by a saltmarsh/desert called the Little Rann of Kutch and from Pakistan by the Great Rann of Kutch and the River Indus delta. Both the Little and the Great Ranns are predominantly flatlands, scattered with elevated mounds or islands, and they support a wide variety of fauna and flora. The Great Rann is known for its huge breeding colony of lesser flamingos (*Phoeniconaias minor*). These pink, long-legged birds hold their bills upside-down in the water and use their tongues to suck in water and mud, filtering the result in their mouths to extract the algae, small insects, and crustaceans. They are noisy gregarious birds but sometimes communicate just by flashing the black feathers on their wings.

The Little Rann and surrounding areas are the only known home of the wild ass (*Equus hemionus khur*) in the Indian peninsula. The entire Little Rann of Kutch serves as the Indian Wild Ass Sanctuary and here grazing herds roam peacefully. If disturbed, however, they can be speedy, sprinting along at up to 31mph (50kph). They are able to maintain a pace of some 15mph (24kph) for up to two hours and occasionally reach a top speed of 43mph (70kph) over short distances, making them the fastest Indian animal. During the mating season, stallions fight vigorously for possession of the mares, rearing up on their hind legs, kicking and biting viciously.

Merchants and herders are found here, mainly nomadic Rabari people, moving their cattle, camels, sheep, and goats to fresh pastures. Mainly Hindus and Jains, the majority of them are

vegetarian and since their religions prohibit the slaughter of livestock, their animals are not butchered or used as draft animals, but serve only to supply milk, ghee (a type of clarified butter), and manure. Any old or weak cattle are cared for in special camps.

The Little Rann of Kutch Wildlife Sanctuary serves to protect the desert region of northwest Gujarat, especially the outer edge and a narrow belt of adjoining land. Wolves roam here – and caracals. These large pale cats have long ears controlled by 20 different muscles and adorned with sensitive tufts of fur that help to locate prey – hares, rodents, young gazelles, and antelopes. Unlike other wild cats, they are relatively easy to tame and have long been used as hunting cats in India. Here too are desert foxes, wild cats, and soaring raptors – tawny eagles and vultures.

Above: A cow waits patiently outside a desert house, hoping to be fed. Many homes here are made from mud and cow dung.

Opposite: The lynx-like caracal is a powerful, long-legged cat with beautiful markings; stiff hairs on its paws function like natural 'sandshoes' that make the going on desert terrain easier. Strong and fast, it can catch small deer and leaps into the air to snatch birds. Other creatures here include wolves, desert cats, and desert gerbils that look like miniature kangaroos.

Above: This vivid fresco on a Jodhpur wall depicts a lavishly dressed elephant ridden by a princely figure. Elephants have often been bejeweled, decorated and draped in rich fabrics for regal occasions. They may also appear as architectural features – in the decorative detailing or as sculpture – as well as in paintings and jewelry.

Opposite: Mehrangarh fort, Jodhpur, founded in 1459, is one of India's largest and most impressive fortresses, set on a lofty height with some sections of its bastioned walls hewn out of the rock itself. It was described by Rudyard Kipling as 'the creation of angels, fairies and giants.'

Blue Jodhpur

In the Indian subcontinent, deserts cover an area of about 87,000sq miles (225,000km²), some seven percent of the total land area. Animals here have to survive periods of intense heat and searing sun with scant water resources and so some rarely drink, relying mainly on the fluids that can be obtained from their prey. Plant seeds can survive for years without water awaiting the moment when the appearance of water sets germination in motion.

Birdlife flourishes, with some very colorful and spectacular specimens being found here. There are sand grouse, partridges, bee-eaters, larks, demoiselle cranes, tawny and steppe eagles, long-legged and honey buzzards, falcons, kestrels, and great Indian bustards, tall long-legged birds with a head like a crown. It lays only a single egg. Fewer than 1000 of these now globally

threatened birds remain – with some 400 making their home in the Thar Desert.

The desert region of northwest India is divided into two regions – the Great Desert and the Little Desert. The Little Desert spreads its sandy frontiers northward from the Luni river between Jaisalmer and Jodhpur. Jodhpur is the largest city in the region, set in scrub forest and often called the Blue City, due to the indigo tint applied to the whitewashed houses here; the color is said to reflect the heat and deter mosquitoes. The jodhpurs that horseriders wear are named after this city, as polo players here once wore this style of trouser.

Jodhpur's Umaid Bhawan Palace is one of the largest residences in the world with 347 rooms, many stately suites, beautiful balconies, courtyards, and fine gardens – a project that employed 3000 artisans over 15 years (between 1929 and 1944). The Art

Deco palace is named after the Maharaja Umaid Singh and is now divided into royal residence, hotel, and museum.

Nearby is Mehrangarh fortress (begun in 1459) set on a rocky cliff that rises high above the desert plains with massive battlements, cannon-guarded ramparts, and monumental gateways studded with spikes to repel military elephant attacks. Behind lies a courtyard with latticed alcoves, carved balconies, gold embroidered Mughal silk tents, and many elegant rooms – one housing fine elephant howdahs – a ballroom, armory, and royal chamber with rich murals and surfaces inlaid with mirror and glass.

Sacred architecture in India is at its very best here with many fine early temples decorated with intricate carvings and sculpture. Often, colorful murals and frescoes depict life in ancient times, mythological characters, or the life of Lord Krishna.

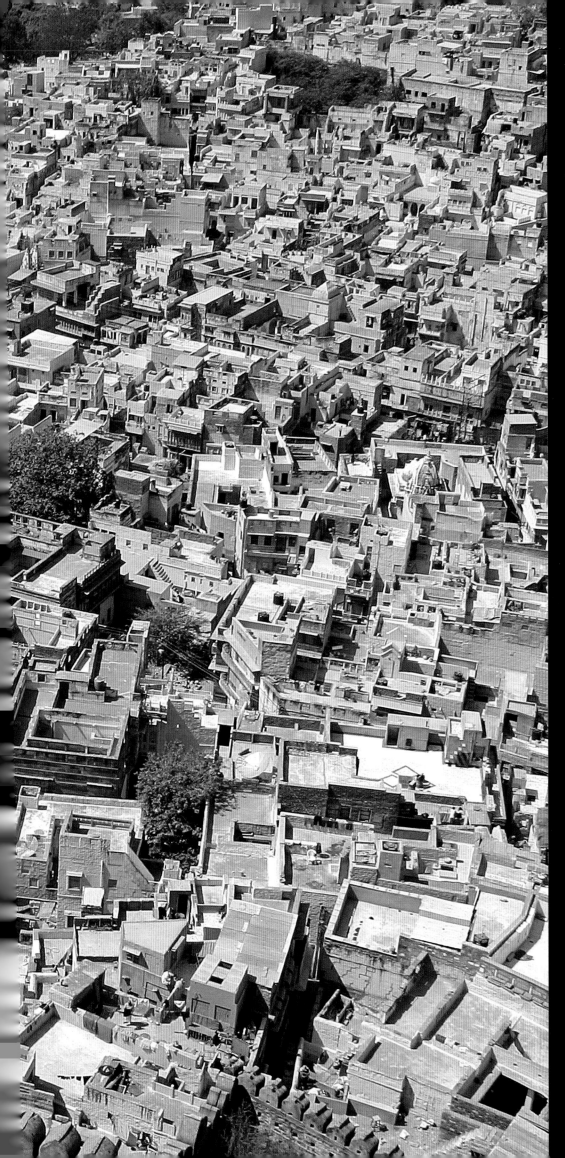

These pages: Founded in 1459, Jodhpur rises like an island in the golden sea of the Thar Desert. Rajasthan's second largest city (after Jaipur) is crowned by the hilltop eyrie of Mehrangarh fort (from where this picture, left, is taken). Its blue haze of buildings has earned Jodhpur the nickname of the Blue City. Initially this azure wash was used to denote a Brahmin residence but soon it became widely popular as people discovered that not only did it reflect the heat away but also seemed to deter mosquitoes.

The Thar Desert

An area of barren rocky waste divides the Little Desert from the Great Desert – the Thar. This is India's main desert region, mostly set in Rajasthan, and extending northward from the edge of the Rann of Kutch salt marshes beyond the Luni river (the only natural water source) to wriggle along the entire Rajasthan-Sind frontier. Some consider it to be up to 10,000 years old, or perhaps even older. Others argue that the area turned to desert relatively recently – perhaps in about 2000 to 1500 BC when the Ghaggar ceased to be a major river (it now expires in the desert). Whatever its origins, today this is the Great Indian Desert and it spreads over two Pakistani states and four Indian states – Punjab, Haryana, Gujarat, and Rajasthan where the shimmering deserts are dotted with majestic forts. It is mainly gently undulating terrain, with shifting sand dunes, numerous isolated hills, and massive fossilized tree trunks.

Scant rain falls between July and September when temperatures may peak at 122°F (50°C) but during January they can plummet to 39°F (4°C) and there are frequent frosts. Dust storms and fierce winds blow at up to 93mph (150kph) in May and June. Yet despite these inhospitable conditions, the Thar is populated with more people than many other deserts. Some 17.44 million people and 23.33 million livestock are recorded as living here. There are ten times more animals per person in Rajasthan than India's national average and overgrazing adds to problems inherent in an area already stricken by drought, winds, and water erosion.

Above and right: Camel safaris are becoming increasingly popular with tourists, providing income to many camel owners, tradespeople, and entertainers in Jaisalmer and nearby villages.

While the northern desert supports some small clumps of thorn forest, acacia trees, tamarix, euphorbias, and several herbs that help to consolidate the surface, the Thar's sandy soil remains dry for a longer period and so is prone to fierce wind erosion that shifts the dust and often blows it onto erstwhile fertile lands.

Unlike the Sahara, there are no palm-fringed oases here. At first glance this appears to be desolate terrain of vast dunes with hillocks, gravel plains, compact salt lake bottoms, and craggy rocks. Despite this arid, unforgiving landscape, however, the desert is home to a variety of wildlife – Bengal foxes, wolves, and desert cats including caracals. There are 25 snake species and 23 lizard species and the region is a haven for migratory and resident birds – harriers, laggar falcons, buzzards, sand grouse, kestrels, vultures, and eagles.

In fact, some wildlife species that are fast vanishing in other parts of India abound here. This is the home of the lesser florican bird (*Eupodotis indica*), black bucks, and Indian gazelles (chinkara). These desert creatures have adapted to survive harsh conditions, soaring temperatures, and scarce water supplies. Some species have evolved to conserve energy by being smaller than their relatives who live in lusher areas – or they may avoid the scorching sun by adopting a nocturnal way of life. Water occurs deep down, 100-400ft (30–120m) below ground level.

One smallish tree that survives – probably as the Thar's only indigenous tree – is the khejri tree (*Prosopis cineraria*). The khejri is considered sacred by the Bishnoi community who live in the desert region of Jodhpur. This evergreen thorny tree provides timber for buildings, wells, fencing, water pipes, tool-handles, boat frames, wheels, and carts. Both leaves and pods are used as fodder for camels, cattle, sheep, goats, and donkeys. There is a popular saying that death will not visit a man, even at the time of a famine, if he has a goat, a camel, and a khejri tree.

In conclusion

Of all the varied landscapes of India, it is perhaps the verdant plains that we envisage when we first think of this colorful nation. The plains are vast areas of green, often well-cultivated land that rolls away from the flanks of mighty rivers which bring vital water and fertility to the soil. The plains encompass centuries of history and culture – they are home to vibrant cities and busy with thousands of inhabitants. By contrast, the arid desert areas are often almost empty zones, but they include some of the nation's most exciting landscapes. Here beautiful palaces rise beside shimmering lakes, and colorful festivals are held among the ever-shifting sand dunes.

Above: *A desert home may be a simple, thatched mud hut.*

Opposite: *Houses here are often painted with depictions of animals, birds, and flowers. A businessman might suspend a string of chili peppers and a lime from his doorway to invite prosperity.*

HILLS AND MOUNTAINS

Much of the subcontinent's landscape is dotted by green hills that offer escape from noisy towns or the hot dusty summer plains. Up here the air is cooler and the lush emerald surroundings are a world away from the city's hustle and bustle. The mountains soar yet higher, with the mighty Himalayas presenting spectacular scenery. Here are awe-inspiring peaks, as well as places of solitude in which to reflect upon the world below and, especially, the amazing nation that is India.

HILLS AND MOUNTAINS

I ndia is a country that is renowned for its contrasting scenery, with diverse landscapes that range from desert to lush jungle, from seacoasts to sweeping plains and from rivers and valleys to gentle hills, soaring mountain ranges, and then the mighty Himalayas where some of the most famous peaks in the world jostle for attention.

Aravali mountains and Jaipur

Rajasthan, in northwest India, is divided into two by the ancient Aravali range which contains some of the world's oldest mountains. It runs northeasterly for about 350 miles (560km) with high peaks, isolated hills, rocky ridges, arid deserts and lush water-filled valleys until its northern end finishes just south of Delhi. Most of the mountains rise between 1000 and 3000ft (300 and 900m) but the highest point is on Mount Abu where a peak called Guru Shikhar reaches 5650ft (1722m).

Above: A man gazes at the sunset at Mount Abu, a romantic hill and lake resort set amid misty and lushly forested hills at the southern tip of the Aravali range. Inspiring temples are found here and the entire hillside is covered with conifers and flowering shrubs.

Right: The Amber fort near Jaipur is a palace complex within a fort – set on a hill and built of red sandstone and white marble. Its construction was begun by Raja Man Singh I in 1592 on the remains of an 11th-century fort but the buildings added by Raja Jai Singh I (ruled 1621–67) are considered to be the most splendid.

Above: There is gorgeous decoration encompassing sparkling mirror details in the Hall of Victory in the Amber Fort (top). Elephants and their mahouts wait in a line, ready to transport tourists up the steep approach to the Amber Fort (center). Visiting school children pose for a photograph at the mighty fort (below).

Nestled amid the Aravali mountains is the capital city of Rajasthan, Jaipur, founded in 1727 by Maharaja Sawai Jai Singh. It is home to much magnificent architecture and was designed and planned by a Bengali architect, Vidyadhar Bhattacharya, with nine rectangular sectors symbolizing the nine divisions of the universe. The region around Jaipur was once a state overrun with hostile factions with many competing warrior kings and so a good number of towering forts were raised here to intimidate the enemy. The Amber Fort, near Jaipur, is a fine example of 16th-century Rajput-Mughal architecture. The red sandstone and white marble palace complex is set at the mouth of a rocky mountain gorge; caparisoned elephants carry visitors up the steep approach ramp. Inside, a vast hall of mirrors can be lit by a single candle, which is reflected from one end to the other.

The city of Jaipur is often called 'the pink city' because of the various shades of pink wash with which people living within city limits are still bound by law to paint their houses. The Palace of the Winds (Hawa Mahal) was built in 1799 by Maharaja Sawai Pratap Singh. It was originally created to offer a vantage point, behind stone-carved screens, from which the court ladies could peep (through more than 900 niches) to observe life in the busy streets and bazaar. Shaped like a crown adorning Lord Krishna's head, the palace offers superb views of the city's fine pink buildings and streets busy with motorcycles and camels.

Above: The Monkey Temple (Galta Ji Mandir) in Galwar Bagh is a Hindu temple complex and pilgrimage site where a local saint brought forth a spring from the Ganges and filled a reservoir with its holy water. There are monkeys everywhere.

Left: Amber fort is set high above Maotha lake.

Above: A pink palace in a pink city – much of Jaipur, founded in 1727, was built in a mere eight years and was designed by Jai Singh II, including the City Palace and the Jantar Mantar, an astronomical observatory. The seven old city gates remain, with one leading into the amazing jewelry market.

Top: Within the Amber Fort, the arches in this cloistered room (once used for open-air meetings) glow with a golden-pink hue. This impressive fort and palace complex is a superb example of Rajput architecture and emerged gradually over a century and a half of fine building work and exceptional craftsmanship.

Right: Hawa Mahal, the Palace of the Winds in Jaipur, is cooled by the breeze drifting through its 953 small windows. The beautifully detailed pink and red sandstone building remains cool even in high summer.

Sanchi's stupas

North of Bhopal in the state of Madhya Pradesh, is the Great Stupa (or Stupa Number One), one of the most elaborate and well known of the 50 or so magnificent Buddhist monuments that crown the hilltop at Sanchi. This is just one element of a complex of structures that were raised between the 3rd century BC to the 2nd century AD. Initially, stupas were burial or reliquary mounds covering the relics of the Buddha or his followers but, in due course, they became symbolic religious edifices or memorials built in holy places. The stupa is the forerunner of the pagoda. Small stupas, sometimes made of crystal, gold, silver, or other precious metals, may house precious religious relics.

Whatever their scale, stupas symbolize the Buddha and his final release from the cycle of birth and rebirth, as well as being a cosmic symbol that represents the world egg. Usually they are set upon a square pedestal and aligned with the four cardinal compass points. Rising above their summits the world's axis is represented as a series of 'parasols,' one above the other to suggest the heavenly hierarchy. A ritual path may encircle the monument.

As well as these stupas, Sanchi boasts many fine examples of Indian Buddhist art and architecture covering some 1500 years. Buddhist monasteries were sited somewhere quiet to allow for peaceful contemplation but because the monks were required to beg for alms each day, they were usually established near to a town or a busy trade route. Sanchi was quiet enough to allow meditation but also usefully near to the prosperous mercantile city of Vidisha.

Left: A Buddhist stupa in the Himalayas – these spiritual monuments were raised to help believers achieve purification and enlightenment. They represent the enlightened mind, with each building section embodying a different Buddhist principle. It is customary to walk around the stupa in contemplation and prayer.

Hill stations

While India was under the sway of colonial rule, the Europeans sought to escape the heat and dust of the northern cities and plains in high summer. They found respite in the cooler hills, especially in the foothills of the Himalayas and the Nilgiri range in Tamil Nadu and Kerala where the air was much fresher. Here they established hill stations – small resorts that provided a nostalgic reminder of life back home, with villas and cottages built in colonial style.

When India gained its independence, most of these country homes were sold to local people and now many welcome tourists during the summer months. Here is greener, lusher vegetation, mist, dew, and a cool refreshing breeze all year round. East Darjeeling, famous for its tea garden, is situated at the edge of the Himalayas. Kalimpong is set amid the gentle slopes and beautiful valleys of the Deolo and Durpin hills, while Gangtok in the state of Sikkim is famous for its ancient ornate monasteries.

As well as the great Himalayas, there are six other significant mountain ranges in India with scattered hill stations in the south, east, and west – each with its own special local foods and festivals. The Western Ghats have many a misty hilly summit while the Eastern Ghats hug the eastern coast parallel to the Bay of Bengal. Munnar boasts the high peak of Anamudi situated in Idukki District of Kerala state, which at a height of 8842ft (2695m) is the highest elevation in southern India. Wayanad highlands with altitudes ranging from 2300 to 7000ft (700 to 2100m) are also found in Kerala, while toward the northwest lie the beautiful hill stations of Rajasthan and Maharashtra.

The British, in particular the British Indian Army, founded some 50 of the 80 or so hill stations; the others were established by Indian rulers over the centuries as places to relax or more temperate surroundings in which to rule – several served as summer capitals of princely states or provinces.

Right: Roads weave a wriggling route through a vast tea plantation in Munnar, Kerala. This is a hill station area where 30 or so tea estates are set in lovely cool countryside with hills and lush grasslands, forests, valleys, and lakes. It is often called 'India's Switzerland.'

Darjeeling

Once long ago, the area around Darjeeling was ruled by the kingdoms of Nepal and Sikkim. In 1828 a delegation of British East India Company officials, staying here en route to Sikkim, were convinced that it would make a wonderful site for a sanitorium for British soldiers so they persuaded the Company to negotiate a lease and soon a hill station was founded here. Darjeeling's temperate climate made it an ideal hill town where British residents could escape the heat of the plains. The town lies at an altitude of about 7000ft (2100m). It is also famous for its tea plantations that date back to 1841 when the British first experimented with growing tea here. Darjeeling is still famous for its special hybrids of black tea with renowned fermenting techniques and fine blends.

The Darjeeling Himalayan Railway opened in 1881, connecting the town with the plains and allowing for the easier transportation of commodities, such as tea and rice. It was the first – and is still the most outstanding – hill passenger railway. Ingenious engineering techniques established a rail link across mountainous terrain. Fully operational and retaining most of its original features, since 1999 it has been afforded UNESCO world heritage status with the services of one of the steam engines still operating in India.

Above: *The narrow gage railway which runs through Darjeeling.*

Right: *Ingenious engineering established rail links across India, including its mountainous terrain. This beautiful old steam locomotive is lovingly cared for; it is bedecked with colorful flags, golden stars, a lion's head, and a brilliant peacock.*

Above: *This seat offers the chance to gaze at an awe-inspiring view. Here the world's third highest mountain, Kanchanjunga, soars to 28,169ft (8586m) as the true showpiece of several spectacular high peaks called the 'Five Treasures of the Great Snow,' each with a summit over 26,246ft (8000m).*

Opposite above: *A beautifully marked clouded leopard. These cats are excellent tree climbers, able to descend headfirst slowly down a vertical trunk. They hunt on the ground as well as in trees, catching small primates and mammals, such as porcupines, deer, and wild boar.*

Singalila National Park

Set in the Darjeeling district of West Bengal, the Singalila park was formed as a wildlife sanctuary in 1986 and became a national park in 1992. This is a popular trekking route. The Singalila Ridge rises to an altitude of over 7000ft (2100m) above sea level. Here are forests of oaks, bamboo, rhododendrons (white, scarlet, pink, and yellow), magnolias, silver firs and junipers, with superb wildflowers such as orchids, geraniums, primulas, saxifrages, cotoneasters, velvety blue iris in the meadows, and stunning Himalayan cobra lilies. Called jack-in-the-pulpits, their tall upright slender spathes rise above striped speckled stems that resemble snakeskin. They thrive in the constant moisture here – either rain or mist. Unfortunately they are poisonous and exude a sap that irritates the skin and eyes. Sandakphu, the loftiest peak of the Singalila Range, is sometimes called the mountain of poisonous plants because of the cobra lilies that flourish here, as well as 600 varieties of orchids.

The park's mammals include leopard cats, clouded leopards, red pandas, barking deer, yellow-throated martens, wild boar, pangolins, pikas, Himalayan black bears, serow (goat-like animals), leopards, chinkara gazelles, and the occasional elephant or tiger. Up above, creatures on the wing include pigeons, doves, cuckoos, hornbills, scarlet minivets, kalij and blood pheasants, brown and fulvous parrotbills, fire-tailed myzornis, and golden-breasted fulvettas. In the breeding season, Himalayan newts congregate around the lakes here, while fat leeches infest the wet ravines.

The Singalila Ridge forms a natural border between Nepal and India. The mountainous terrain is criss-crossed by innumerable streams. A subtropical humid climate allows tree growth beyond the snowline – unlike the Western Himalayas. There are magnificent views of Kanchanjunga, the third highest mountain in the world (after Mount Everest and K2) with an altitude of 28,169ft (8586m).

Above: A goat-like serow with sharp pointed horns stands in a bleak snowy forest. It eats grass, shoots, and leaves, feeding at dawn and dusk on the rugged Himalayan slopes, establishing regular tracks. It is sometimes seen at an altitude of 12,000ft (3650m).

Nilgiris – the Blue Mountains

This range of mountains in southern India crosses the states of Tamil Nadu and Kerala. The Doda Betta peak is, at 8652ft (2637m), the highest point in Tamil Nadu. Here there are valleys, glades, sudden escarpments, and hill stations. At the Mudumalai Wildlife Sanctuary (a continuation of the Bandipur National Park) hills, valleys, ravines, watercourses, and swamps provide fertile ground for tropical moist deciduous forests, dry deciduous and scrub forests with bamboos, natural teak, and many blossoming shrubs and flowering plants.

The wildlife includes elephants, tigers, leopards, langurs, bonnet macaques, wild dogs, mugger crocodiles, sloth bears, gaur, spotted and mouse deer, wild boar, porcupines, mongooses, otters, and giant flying squirrels. Soaring above are gray hornbills, hawks, buzzards, harriers, falcons, crested hawk eagles – and the crested serpent eagle (*Spilornis cheela*). This, as its name suggests, hunts snakes and lizards; it perches on the trees to scan the world below. Its large head and hood give it a rather owl-like appearance. Other birds include peacocks, gray partridge, quails, goggle-eyed plovers, gray bulbuls, and mynahs.

Above: *Tea pickers on an estate in Nilgiris, an area with many sprawling tea plantations set amid the rolling hills that produce a dark, intensely aromatic tea. There are mountains too and lush valleys where waterfalls plummet from the heights.*

Right: *A family of shaggy-haired sloth bears – they have white U- or Y-shaped chest markings, a pale muzzle, large lips, and long tongues designed to slurp up ants and termites that their hook-like claws are adapted to dig out of nests.*

The Nilgiris and the south Western Ghats are areas where a good number of tigers roam. Each tiger boasts a unique pattern of more than 100 stripes and (as veterinary surgeons have discovered) their blue-toned skin is striped too, not just their fur. The fascinating pattern of stripes on a tiger's forehead often takes the form of the Chinese 'wang' mark, denoting a king.

Except when mothers are rearing cubs, tigers usually live alone but their territories can overlap and most tigers mark their favorite sites by spraying a mix of urine and scent-gland secretions on trees and bushes, and by making deep longitudinal scratches on trunks with sharp claws that are at least 3 to 4in (80 to 100mm) long. Special glands between the tiger's toes produce secretions that also mark trees with chemical scent signals, readily distinguished by other tigers. Tigers also use their sharp talons for grooming their coats, removing dead hair, tangles, and any irritating parasites. When tigers pounce on their prey, their hooked claws enable them to grasp the animal's skin firmly and prevent its escape.

Bandhavgarh National Park in Madhya Pradesh is named after an ancient fort and is set in the Vindhya mountain range of central India. It is said to have the highest density of tigers in India and its forests were once the home of the elusive white tiger. None of these magnificent creatures has been spotted in the wild for 50 years or so and less than a dozen have been seen in India during the last 100 years, but it was here in Bandhavgarh that they were recorded. Once a hunting reserve of the royal family of Rewa, this area was declared a national park in 1968.

Above and left: In daylight, a tiger's sight is comparable to human vision but at night, when tigers hunt, it is six times better than ours.

From forest to alpine slopes

Once upon a time, tropical moist deciduous forest covered all of the sub-Himalayan area while, in the Middle Himalayas between 5000 and 12,000ft (1520 to 3660m) pines, oaks, poplars, walnuts, larches and rhododendrons grew. However, these woodlands have been subject to such great deforestation that now they survive only on the most inaccessible, steepest slopes.

In the higher parts of the Great Himalayas, just below the snowline, alpine vegetation includes shrubs, rhododendrons, mosses, lichens, edelweiss, and stunning wildflowers such as the unique and startlingly colored Himalayan blue poppy that stands etched against the rocky terrain.

Pygmy hogs (*Sus salvanius*) are the smallest and rarest wild pigs in the world and they live in the foothills of the Himalayas in northwest Assam, in tall savannah grasslands where their dark brown coats provide excellent camouflage. Once thought to be extinct, these tiny pigs were rediscovered in 1971.

The sub-Himalayan foothills were once home to many tigers, leopards, rhinoceroses, and deer but today these creatures are restricted to special protected areas, such as the Jaldapara and Kaziranga sanctuaries, respectively found in West Bengal and Assam. In the Great Himalayas, musk deer, wild goats, sheep, wolves, and snow leopards are found.

Above: *Wild flowers bloom alongside high altitude mountain lakes.*

Right: *Horses graze beside a rushing river below the high peaks of the rugged Himalays.*

The top of the world

Up in the north rise the awe-inspiring Himalayas where coniferous forests give way to dry alpine scrub, soaring peaks, and the deep snow of the world's highest mountains. In Sanskrit, the name Himalayas means 'abode of snow.' The mountains form a continuous curve for nearly 1550 miles (2500km) along the northern edge of the Indian subcontinent, in an arc that ranges from about 125 to 250 miles (200 to 400km) wide as it sweeps across from the Indus river in the northwest to the Brahmaputra river in the east. The mountains, which comprise more than 110 peaks, rise abruptly from the Gangetic plain and then drop again to the Tibetan plateau to the north.

This is the world's highest mountain region. It boasts many of the tallest peaks in the world including the impressive trio of Mount Everest at 29,028ft (8848m), K2 or Mount Godwin Austen at 28,251ft (8611m) and Kanchanjunga at 28,169ft (8586m) – this last being in India. Other awe-inspiring peaks in India include Nanda Devi at 25,646ft (7817m).

Often referred to as the queen of mountains, spectacular Kanchanjunga has multiple ecological zones that range from subtropical up to icy wilderness and the mighty Kanchanjunga glacier. Its highest peak is encircled by others and the huge massif is buttressed by great ridges that contain a host of peaks from 19,685 to 26,250ft (6000 to 8000m) high. Its name translates as 'the five treasuries of snows' after five of these splendid peaks – four are over 27,723ft (8450m) high; three are on the border of North Sikkim and two in Taplejung, district in eastern Nepal.

Until 1852, Kanchanjunga was believed to be the world's highest peak but calculations following an 1849 survey proclaimed that Mount Everest was, in fact, the highest and that Kanchanjunga now ranked third. It was first scaled by a British expedition led by Charles Evans in 1955 when Joe Brown and George Band honored local beliefs that the summit is sacred to a protective deity and stopped just a few feet short of this point, a tradition that has been observed ever since by climbers who followed in their wake.

The Kanchanjunga National Park comprises wet temperate forests at the lower levels, rising to bare rock, ice, and snow at the mountain summits. Because of its inhospitable location, the Kanchanjunga area remains rarely visited and pristine. The Zemu Glacier here – the largest in the Eastern Himalayas – is one place where a long line of mysterious footprints are said to have been reported by Sir John Hunt, leader of the Everest Expedition in 1953. These contributed to rumors about the possible presence here of the 'abominable snowman,' or yeti.

Sikkim, India's second smallest state, is set entirely in rugged snow-clad mountains. The Lepchas were its earliest settlers. The Bhutias arrived from Tibet in the 1300s while many Nepalis settled here during the 1700s and 1800s. These people of the mountains mainly follow Tibetan Buddhism and Hinduism. Like so much of India, the capital, Gangtok, is a blend of ancient and modern, where multi-story buildings rise alongside traditional homes, stupas, and monasteries and where Buddhist monks can be seen in their bright saffron and maroon robes. Gangtok is the only capital city in India to boast a cable car.

To the east of Gangtok, and close to India's border post with China, lies the serene Tsomgo Lake at 12,139ft (3700m) which remains frozen for most of the year. However, in mid-summer it is surrounded by rhododendrons, primulas, irises, and poppies that bloom along its banks and nearby hillsides. The largest lake in Sikkim is Gurudogmar; this is one of the highest lakes in the Himalayas at an altitude of about 17,200ft (5240m) and it is frozen over in winter except for one spot, which the devout believe is especially blessed.

Above: Shivling peak in the Garhwal Himalayan range has a similar, pyramid shape to Switzerland's Matterhorn. Its steep rock faces glisten with snow and ice as they rise above the Gangotri glacier.

Opposite: Dzongri in south Sikkim is a popular trekking destination where dramatic snow-covered mountain peaks rise on all sides, some to over 20,000ft (6000m).

The Great Himalayan National Park

Set amid the towering western Himalayas that rise on three sides, in the beautiful district of Kullu in Himachal Pradesh state are temperate and virgin coniferous forests. Oaks, blue pines, spruce, and silver birches thrive as well as vast areas of high alpine pastures and glaciers. Here, in a park created in 1984, there are waterfalls everywhere, as well as streams and superb wildflowers including geraniums, Himalayan blue poppies, and cobra lilies. Vast numbers of wonderful creatures and plants thrive here, many in sacred groves protected by the people who believe in the special qualities of these places.

The park encompasses a range of altitudes from about 4900 to 19,700ft (1500 to 6000m). Here rise awe-inspiring snowcapped mountains and steep rugged cliffs casting purple shadows over deep river valleys. There are broadleaved woodlands of oak and bamboo as well as pine forests and alpine meadows pinpricked with vivid wildflowers.

The highly endangered Himalayan musk deer (*Moschus chrysogaster*) roams here. (The black musk deer [*Moschus fuscus*] lives in the eastern Himalayas.) The petite Himalayan musk deer is about 2ft (60cm) tall with a shoulder height of only 8in (20cm) and it has long hare-like ears. It has a hairless tail with

a small tuft at the end and long upper canines that show even when its mouth is closed. The musk sac is external and lies between its reproductive organs and umbilicus. The strong-smelling secretion produced by this organ has been used in perfumes and the traditional medicine of China for over 5000 years but this is now an illegal trade pursued only by poachers. Unfortunately the continuing incidence of poaching is endangering the population of musk deer.

Here too are sleek leopards (including the rare snow leopard). There are Himalayan black bears, brown bears, langurs, rhesus macaques, and wild sheep – Himalayan thar and bharal – as well as ibex and serow antelopes. A rich bird life of 68 resident and some 50 migrant species includes glorious brightly colored pheasants, such as the beautiful monal (*Lophophorus impejanus*) with its glossy blue, red, and gold feathers and the superbly spotted Western tragopan (*Tragopan melanocephalus*) with deep crimson throat and neck and black cap to its head.

Above: *Close to the ice-capped Himalayan peaks is Manali, with its forest-clad valleys; here the rocks are covered in green moss.*

Opposite: *Near to its source, the river Ganges surges through a dramatic steep-sided and rather forbidding canyon.*

Nanda Devi

Overlooked by India's second highest peak, this is an area of unspoiled forest with alpine pastures and the famous Valley of Flowers National Park, bursting with some 500 vascular plants and over 80 bird species, such as rosefinches, pipits, and bush warblers. Nanda Devi National Park overall has 112 bird species including colorful pheasants, plus snow partridges and snowcocks high up in the alpine meadows and on barren rocky slopes. This is essentially wilderness, a largely inaccessible region with spectacular gorges and sharp ridges.

There are bears, macaques, red foxes, weasels, and Hanuman langurs, which are revered as the descendants of the Hindu monkey god, Hanuman, and so often seen as a temple monkey but here enjoying alpine forests. Superb snow leopards survive in the remotest regions, feasting on musk deer, Himalayan tahr, and blue sheep that have a silvery bluish sheen to improve their camouflage against the rock face when they scamper up precipitous cliffs to escape predators such as leopards, mountain foxes, and tawny eagles.

The Indian Himalayas are at their most dramatic here; great peaks rise majestically, separated by some of the mightiest rivers of northern India. This is an awe-inspiring spot that has given rise to many legends and where the Gangotri glacier is a traditional site of pilgrimage for Hindus as it is revered as the source of the river Ganges. With spectacular flourish, snow and ice contort into cones, pyramids, fans, bridges, serrated crests, ice walls and sometimes great plunging crevasses. All around are crags, glacial lakes, and waterfalls. This is not a single valley glacier, but a combination of several glaciers that meet to form a huge ice mass.

Right: The Gangotri is one of the largest glaciers in the Himalayas and is the source of the sacred river Ganges. It is a pilgrimage site revered for being the seat of the goddess Ganga, the daughter of heaven, whose temple is visited by many pilgrims between May and October. By November, Gangotri is covered in snow.

Mountains and snow leopards

Among this multitude of towering mountain ranges, river valleys, and high plateaus, the traditional culture derived from Tibetan Buddhism survives and many ancient monasteries are maintained in the villages. Buddhist temples (gompas) and stupas are often set upon prominent outcrops and hilltops. Small towns like Leh grew from trading posts to market centers and are now tourist staging posts in mountains that provide a perfect environment for blue sheep, ibex, wolves, wild yaks, and swooping or hovering birds of prey such as the golden eagle and bearded vulture.

The elusive snow leopard (*Uncia uncia*) is an elegant and fearsome creature and the only truly high mountain cat, with a long muscular body and broad paws that carry it effortlessly over the snow. Its pads are covered with fur for protection against ice and cold. The thick tail can be up to 35in (90cm) long and helps to provide balance when this agile cat leaps from ledge to ledge or over ravines, sometimes spanning 46ft (14m) or so in a single jump. This furry tail also serves to protect its nose and mouth from the severest cold temperatures when it wraps it around itself when it settles to sleep. The backs of the leopard's short ears are black except for a spot on each – they are set centrally or near the tip to suggest a pair of eyes to ward off intruders.

The snow leopard lives in mountainous meadows and rocky regions at altitudes of up to 19,700ft (6000m) but in winter it will descend to about 6500ft (2000m) to the forests. Its long dense fur provides essential protection against the cold and may be straw-colored, gray, or chestnut with white on its throat, chest, belly, and inner limbs. The pelt turns white all over in winter but still retains beautiful ringed spots and rosettes. Snow leopards may kill animals up to three times their size, sometimes ambushing prey like ibex and goats from above. They will also eat bharal (blue sheep), musk deer, marmots, hares, and birds, keeping a low profile away from the skyline as they stalk the next meal in a land where food is all too scarce.

Above: On the Tibetan border, Ladakh is a remote mountain region on a Kashmir plateau. Vegetation is extremely sparse in this high altitude desert but mountain sheep, ibex, and yaks scratch out a living here.

Opposite: The elegant, lithe snow leopard has a long tail that provides extra balance in difficult terrain and also serves as vital protection for its nose and mouth when it settles to sleep in freezing conditions. Sadly, as tigers become rarer, hunters now also seek out this endangered, secretive cat for its beautiful (and valuable) deep-pile spotted fur coat.

Red pandas

With bushy striped tails, long whiskers, and black-and-white face markings, the red panda (*Ailurus fulgens*) looks rather like a raccoon – one of their many common names is the Himalayan raccoon. They live in northeastern India, in cool temperate mountain forests with a bamboo understory where they survive almost exclusively on bamboo leaves, supplementing their diet with the young leaves of other plants, blossoms, fruit, berries, grains, nuts, and birds' eggs. They usually live at altitudes of between 5000 to 15,700ft (1500 and 4800m).

Their paws have extended pads and retractable claws that enable them to firmly grasp branches, stems, and twigs as they scramble swiftly up the trees. It is sometimes called a wah because of its distinctive cry. Less than 2500 adults survive in the wild and this beautiful animal ranks among the most severely threatened of the world's rarest creatures.

Above: Red pandas have an amazing number of different names including the Himalayan raccoon, wah (like its cry), red cat, bear cat, cloud bear, fox bear, red fox, fire fox, fire cat, bright panda, small panda, petit panda, and poonya.

Left: The Ganges river flows through Rishikesh, famous as a yoga and meditation center where many, including stars such as the Beatles, Donovan, and Kate Winslet, have come to contemplate and meditate. This is the 'Gateway to the Himalayas' where the mountains rise dramatically as the river rushes onward.

The mountain people

These fearsome altitudes could scarcely be deemed hospitable but nearly 40 million people inhabit the Himalayas. Those who have made their homes here have, over the centuries, had to adapt to harsh living conditions in remote and isolated valleys. Long ago, the indigenous shamanistic cults were challenged by Hinduism emerging from the south, and then, from the 11th century onward, Buddhism from the north. However, within these great mountains, religions cohabit and influence one another so that the shaman has retained a powerful influence, and is still consulted for healing, divination, and to appease hostile spirits.

After India's independence in 1947, communications and local services improved and so did the opportunity for education. Gradually the hill cultures absorbed 20th-century influences and now the literacy rate has increased considerably. However, life in this difficult terrain remains simple and tough – especially in the most remote areas that are cut off by winter snows. A rich cultural legacy survives here that has given rise to countless legends and myths, as well as colorful fairs and festivals that continue the old traditions. The great peaks have hitherto isolated communities and customs from one another but this natural barrier, that in the past has often proved stronger than formal state boundaries, has recently been undermined as satellites speed up communication and bring television reception to the remotest regions. Inevitably, this will impact upon the strong social structure here and the long-surviving cultures. Outside influences have already begun to erode traditional and religious values.

Over and above the physical divisions, the Indian Himalayas rise just where Asia's three main religions converge: the Trans-Himalayan region has long been dominated by Buddhism; Kashmir, especially in the west, is greatly influenced by Islam; the foothills of Jammu, Himachal Pradesh, and Uttar Pradesh form the northern boundary of Hinduism – with the sub-Himalayas being home to many Hindus of Indian heritage (as are the central Himalayan valleys from eastern Kashmir to Nepal). In Himachal Pradesh, the people of Kinnaur have traditionally been referred to as Kinners, encompassing Rajputs (or Khosias) that include Hindus and Buddhists, and Berus that have four artist castes: Lohar, Badhi, Koli, and Nangalu.

Tibetan Buddhists inhabit the Great Himalayas from Ladakh (in the state of Jammu and Kashmir) to northeast India. Indian and Tibetan cultures have intermingled in central Nepal, while the

Above: A Hindu holy man; some live as hermits in the most remote locations. Hindu ascetics (called sadhus) often wear ocher garments, symbolizing renunciation.

Top: In high mountains, the villagers practice ancient farming methods in areas often cut off from 'civilization' during winter.

Opposite: A woman carries water on her head in a large pot, carefully taking this precious resource back to her Himalayan home. Sometimes villagers must walk considerable distances, up and down steep mountain foothills, to reach springs and other water sources.

animistic people of the eastern Himalayas in India (like the animistic peoples of China) adhere to the belief that animals, plants, minerals, and inanimate objects are inhabited by spirits.

Pilgrims have long visited the major Hindu and Buddhist sacred places in the mountains and now tourism too brings its own 'spin-off' employment as visitors arrive to enjoy mountain trekking, wildlife viewing, and climbing. Porters (and pack animals) serve their needs in the most remote areas while other highland people continue to graze their herds in the high meadows in summer. Local women still wear ghagra skirts, traditional headgear, bangles, and heavy ear and nose-rings.

Water for cooking, washing, and drinking must be fetched and carried along narrow mountain paths. Women plow and grow what they can on the banks of the rivers and the terraced hills above, cultivating potatoes, onions, corn, barley, mustard, and a few sturdy apricot and peach trees, while the men often seek work on the plains where it is easier to grow crops.

Northern India is known for its tandoori-style cooking and typical dishes include spicy meatballs or koftas, and meats braised in creamy sauces of yogurts and fruits (kormas). Naan bread or basmati rice may be eaten but in wheat-growing areas, it is bread that is the main source of starch. Many religious sects are vegetarian and cows especially, are considered sacred. The practice of vegetarianism in India stretches back to the rise of Buddhism and Jainism that preached non-violence to all creatures.

High in the mountains, the fare is perforce simple. Breakfast may consist of hot milk and thick chapatis stuffed with minced radish. Other meals will inevitably involve many different kinds of dhal (a spicy stew made from pulses) cooked in enormous cooking pots that bubble away atop large log fires – one delicious variety is made with mustard seed and dates.

The traditional Himalayan home has two or three stories – the lowest filled with stones to improve its stability should an earthquake strike. Floor two accommodates the livestock while the family live at the top. The building fabric is stone and wood or it may be raised on bricks of sun-dried mud.

Above: Shimla (top), capital of Himachal Pradesh in the northwest Himalayas, has been called the 'Queen of Hill Stations.' This colorful busy market (center) is in Leh, the part of Ladakh district in Jammu and Kashmir state. A modest village house in Ladakh (below); this arid area lies within the rain shadow of the Great Himalayas.

Above: Sheep and goats beside a Ladakh lake, a treeless desert area below snow-swathed mountains. This challenging environment is the habitat of brown bears, marmots, wild sheep — including the bharal (blue sheep) — and yaks that clamber nimbly over the rough terrain.

Left: The placid domestic yak has a ragged shaggy coat lying over a dense undercoat of soft close-matted hair that helps to retain warmth. It has wide-set curved horns and is considerably smaller than the wild yak.

Following pages: Pilgrims trek to the Holy Amarnath cave in Kashmir. It was here that Lord Shiva explained the secrets of immortality to his consort Parvati, and was overheard by two white doves that thus gained eternal life. Pilgrims often report seeing doves here. Set 13,100ft (4000m) high, the ice cave is covered with snow for most of the year.

Holy places

The vital thread of religion weaves a pattern through the lives of ordinary people, as well as pilgrims and holy men. Some caves in the Himalayas are said to be sacred and many have become the homes of sages and Buddhist monks who have chosen to meditate in these ancient sanctuaries, undoubtedly inspired by the peace and drama of their surroundings, by many a glorious sunrise and the crisp exhilarating mountain air.

Pilgrims sometimes visit the caves, some of which are famous for mystical echoing effects similar to those described in the incident that occurs in the Marabar Caves in E. M. Forster's novel *A Passage to India*. Many caves are inhabited by sadhus; these ascetics or practitioners of yoga are holy men who have renounced worldly attachments and who spend their days in devotion to their chosen deity. Some seek liberation through meditation and contemplation in a place where the mountain peaks are dedicated to deities. The Himalayas have been revered as the abode of divinity since the dawn of India's religions.

Badrinath in Uttaranchal state, some 10,248ft (3123m) above sea level, is a Hindu holy town that is the setting for a famous temple devoted to Vishnu at one of the holiest sites marking the four cardinal religious points of India to which pilgrimages are made. The other sites are at Rameswaran in Tamil Nadu in the south, Puri in Orissa in the east and Dwarka in Gujarat in the west. Here in Badrinath, despite its remote location between the Nar and Narayana mountain ranges, the temple attracts some 600,000 pilgrims a year.

Many also visit Kedarnath that lies amid the Garhwal Himalayas at the head of the Mandakini river. This has a most holy Hindu

temple and shrine. The present temple was erected in the 700s but was set beside the site of an even earlier place of worship. Kedar is another name for the protector and destroyer, Lord Shiva, and outside the temple is a vast stone statue of the holy Nandi Bull, Lord Shiva's vehicle.

Opposite: *This magnificent white-domed stupa in Ladakh is set amid the winter ice and snow in one of the highest and coldest deserts in the world.*

Above: *The winter snows have melted away. A stream of brightly colored prayer flags flutter and snap against an azure sky in Ladakh as the sun warms each craggy rockface.*

These pages: Many temples and monasteries here are embellished with brilliant imagery: the enigmatic gaze of Buddha (top); the monkey god Hanuman with Prince Rama's wife, Sita (center); a vivid Buddhist fresco (above). A boy holds a prayer wheel while he studies at 10th-century Lamayuru Monastery, set on a steep Himalayan mountain in Ladakh (right).

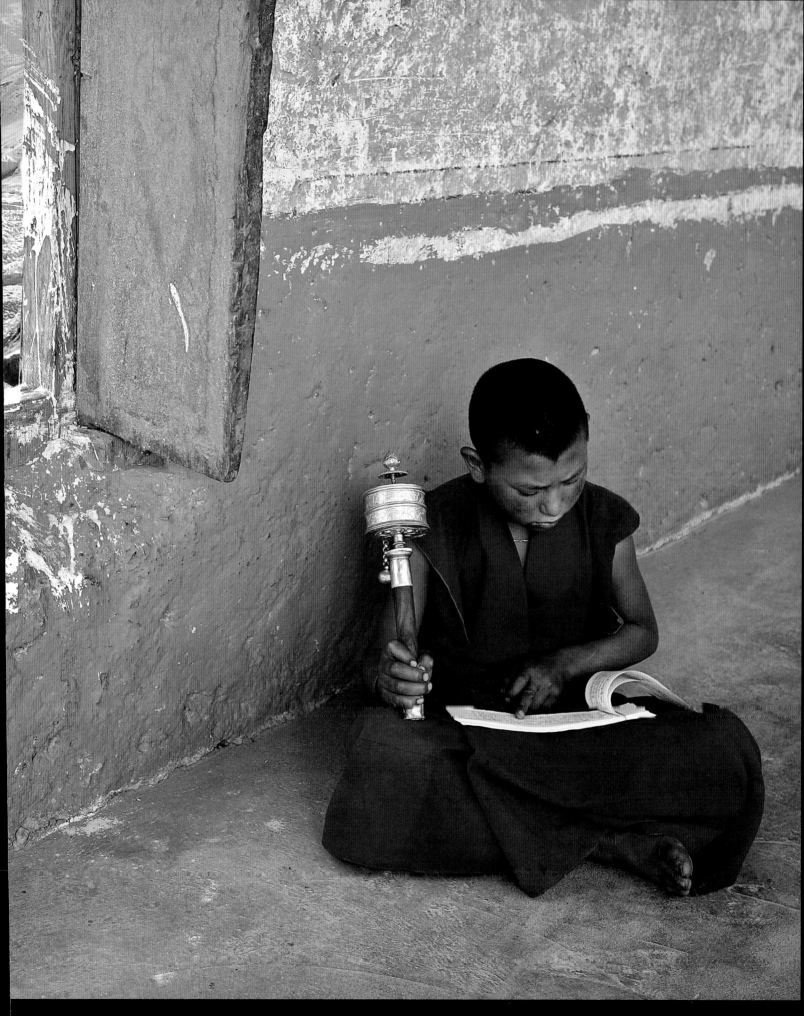

The roof of India

This part of India is a place of soaring peaks, of glacial streams and frozen lakes, of ancient monasteries and deep, mysterious caves. There are pagoda-style temples like Sarahan with its wonderful carved tiger; there are stupas and spires as well as pristine forests, full of extraordinary wildlife. This is the summit of India where wonderful animals, like the snow leopard and the brilliant monal pheasant, survive at the 'roof of the world.' Everest glints in the distance beyond India's own equally awe-inspiring peaks.

This place is indeed a meeting point for many different peoples, for many mountains and faiths, for rich and poor ... and, as it so dramatically marks the northern rim of this stunningly diverse nation, is a fitting point to end our travels. We leave on a real high, as this is both a physical and emotional summit where the land and spirit of India peak!

Above: An impressive view of the Himalayas from Tapoban – set opposite the snow-capped Shivling peak, which, in turn, is guarded by the Bhagirathi range behind.

Right: The sun begins to set as another day in India draws to a close. Here, in the shadow of the sharp peak of Shivling, and in the plains, and in all the cities, ports and villages, far below and far away, night falls.

FASCINATING FACTS

This amazing country gives rise to many equally amazing facts. Figures do vary,
and some are subject to change, but the information on the following pages provides
a few intriguing insights into this remarkable nation. There are so many facets to
India; it is like spinning a diamond and seeing the light blaze into a myriad images
– tigers stalking their prey, pilgrims bathing in the rippling water of the river
Ganges, snow sparkling on a mountain peak, the sun dancing on desert sands or city
lights all a-dazzle.

Learning and knowledge

• The art of navigation was established in India over 6000 years ago: the words 'navy' and 'navigation' are derived from the Sanskrit words 'nou' and 'navgatih.'

• Ancient Indian texts show a remarkably advanced knowledge of anatomy, embryology, digestion, metabolism, and physiology.

• 6th-century BC Sushruta is regarded as the world's first surgeon: he conducted complicated procedures, such as cataract operations, creating artificial limbs, undertaking caesarean deliveries, mending fractures, and cosmetic and brain surgery. He practiced his medicine on the banks of the Ganges near the present-day city of Varanasi.

• The first-ever 'plastic surgery' was undertaken in India over 2600 years ago to replace noses that were commonly cut off as a punishment.

• In about 300 BC, Charaka was one of the founders of ancient India's renowned Ayurveda school of medicine.

• Indian mathematicians invented the number system plus algebra, trigonometry, and calculus.

• The zero was invented by mathematician and astronomer Aryabhata (born in Kerala in AD 476). His work profoundly influenced the course of mathematics in India for centuries to come.

• The 'decimal system' was developed here in 100 BC.

• 6th-century Indian mathematician Budhayan, is credited with calculating the value of 'pi' with great precision.

• Albert Einstein said, 'We owe a lot to the Indians, who taught us how to count, without which no worthwhile scientific discovery could have been made.'

Parks, reserves and animals

• Over 90 national parks cover an area of about 14,900 sq miles (38,569km²), with nearly 500 smaller wildlife sanctuaries occupying about 45,204sq miles (117,077km²).

• India has 14 biosphere reserves (large areas of natural habitat that are protected by law) and 27 tiger reserves.

• Hunting and forest destruction have reduced tiger populations from hundreds of thousands a century ago to probably less than 3000 now.

• A tiger's roar can be heard as far as 2 miles (3km) away.

• Only about 2400 Indian rhinos survive today.

• Despite weighing 4400lb (2000kg), the Indian rhino can charge at 38mph (48kph).

Above: The gharial can grow to an amazing 19ft (6m) in length.

Above left: Blue-streaked painting of sacred cattle on a wall in Udaipur.

Opposite: Wary eyes ever alert for danger, timid deer enter the water.

• It is estimated that between 26,000 and 42,000 Asian elephants currently survive in the wild.

• Asian elephants are more easily tamed than their larger African counterparts and have served as beasts of burden for centuries. They have been ridden into war and still work in India's logging industry.

• Asian elephants can survive in arid places that experience less than 15in (40cm) of annual rainfall, and also in wet areas where over 26ft (8m) of rain may pour down each year.

• India is home to nearly 1200 species of birds.

• The gharial (*Gavialis gangeticus*) lives in the calmer backwaters of rivers in North India. At a glance this primitive creature looks like a crocodile but it has a long, very narrow snout. The gharial eats mainly fish so does not need the heavy muscular jaws of other crocodilians. Its stunted legs mean that it can only crawl when it emerges now and then to bask on mud flats and banks – or to lay eggs. The population of gharials is in serious decline and it is the first crocodilian species to be categorized as critically endangered.

• The Indus River dolphin (*Platanista gangetica minor*) has a long beak, stocky body, and minute eyes that seem no more than pinhole openings without lenses. It is sometimes described as being blind but it can detect the direction and intensity of a light source. It once ranged from the Himalayan foothills to the Indus delta but now, in part because of the new dams and barrages that have been constructed, just three small subpopulations survive; it is one of the world's rarest mammals.

• The Gangetic or Ganges river dolphin (*Platanista gangetica*) is now very rare. It is primarily found where the Ganges and Brahmaputra rivers and their tributaries flow slowly between the plains of India and Bangladesh. Like its counterpart in the Indus, it is virtually blind, probably because it inhabits extremely murky waters where it homes in on fish and invertebrates using echolocation, as well as feeling with its sensitive snout and flippers to probe in the muddy bottom.

• The snake is a common symbol in Indian mythology and Hinduism. Some of these mythical reptiles are viewed as protectors, and others as destroyers. Lord Shiva is generally depicted with a cobra around his neck while Lord Vishnu rests on a seven-headed snake.

Politics, people, religion, and sport

• India can claim to be the largest democracy in the world. It encompasses 28 states and 7 union territories.

• New Delhi is India's capital: here temperatures soar to 113°F (45°C) in May and June.

• While there are only 14 official languages, over 400 languages are spoken here – 24 of them by at least one million people and 114 by over 10,000 voices. It is thought that there may be as many as 844 spoken dialects.

Land, river, and sea

• The entire coastline of India measures about 4670 miles (7516km).

• India's frontier of some 9445 miles (15,200km) lies all in the north where the country borders Pakistan, China and Tibet, Nepal, Bhutan, Bangladesh, and Myanmar (Burma).

• India occupies 1.27 million sq miles (3.29 million km²).

• India occupies only 2.4 percent of the globe's land area but supports over 15 percent of its population.

• The Ganga river basin is India's largest, encompassing some 25 percent of the nation's area.

• Of all India's rivers, the Brahmaputra flows with the greatest volume of water.

• The river Ganga (Ganges) is regarded as holy and so babies are baptized in it. The cremated remains of many Hindus are put into the river in a ceremony that is believed to cleanse their souls.

• The Indian Ocean covers about one-fifth of the total ocean area of the world, stretching for more than 6200 miles (10,000km) between Africa and Australia and covering an area of 28,360,000 sq miles (73,440,000km²).

• Kanchanjunga is India's highest mountain and the third highest in the world at 28,169ft (8586m). Of its five peaks, four stand taller than 27,723ft (8450m) high.

Above: Women in bright saris join a ceremony at Chittorgarh, Rajasthan.

Above left: Varanasi's Ganges riverbanks bustle with people and boats.

Opposite: Polished stone prayer mats gleam in the Taj Mahal mosque.

• Some 70 percent of India's people live in more than 550,000 villages that stretch across the subcontinent and outlying islands.

• The name 'India' is derived from the River Indus, in the valleys around which the homes of the earliest settlers were established. The Indus is now principally found within Pakistan's borders.

• India has seven major religions. Hinduism is the dominant faith, observed by some 82 percent of the population. More than 10 percent (some 138 million) follow Islam and India has one of the world's largest Muslim populations. About 5 percent are Sikhs and Christians; the other 45 million or so are Buddhists, Jains, Bahai, or adherents to other sects.

• Mahatma Gandhi led the Indian independence movement in the first half of the 20th century, and ever since has been associated with peaceful, non-violent protest. He said that, 'Suffering cheerfully endured ceases to be suffering and is transmuted into an ineffable joy.' When asked what he thought of Western civilization, Gandhi memorably replied, 'I think it would be an excellent idea.'

• India's national sport is field hockey for which it has won eight Olympic gold medals – but cricket remains the most popular game.

• The world's highest cricket ground (and polo pitch) is at Chail, in Himachal Pradesh, at over 8000ft (2440m).

Miscellany

• 13th-century saint and poet Gyandev created the game of snakes and ladders. Originally called 'Mokshpat' the ladders represented virtues as the way to heaven, while the snakes represented vices!

• The highest bridge in the world is the 98ft (30m) long Baily Bridge in the Himalayas built by the Indian Army in 1982 at an altitude of about 18,379ft (5602m).

• The rupee is India's currency. This was one of the first places where coins were issued (c.6th century BC). In due course, the word rupee was derived from the term *rup* or *rupa*, which means 'silver' in many Indo-Aryan languages.

• The Taj Mahal was declared one of the seven wonders of the world in July 2007. It was built over 22 years from 1631 to 1653 at an estimated cost of 35 million rupees by 20,000 artisans under the control of Shah Jahan. Legends claim that he wanted the hands of the craftsmen and architect to be cut off afterward so that they could never repeat this wonder.

• Archaeological finds suggest that over 4000 years ago in the Indus Valley, people built brick homes with private baths – and women wore lipstick.

• India has more post offices than any other nation.

• India's vast railway network employs over a million people.

• The railway station with the longest name here is Sri Venkatanarasimharajuvariapeta in Tamil Nadu. The shortest station name is Ib in Orissa.

• Bollywood (the name is a fusion of Hollywood and Bombay – now Mumbai) is the globe's largest film industry. Launched in 1899 when a film was made and shown by means of Edison's projecting kinetoscope, the first of India's silent movies was created here in 1913.

• Collectively, India's film fans go out to the cinema about 3 billion times a year and India produces more movies than any other nation of the world – with Bollywood taking the prize as the globe's largest film industry.

• India is the largest grower and consumer of chilies in the world. It grows more than any other country and consumes over 90 percent of the crop, exporting the rest globally.

INDEX

Picture Credits

(l=left, r=right, a=above, b=below, c=center, i=inset)